The Plays of Mahesh Dattani

A Critical Response

THE PLAYS OF
Mahesh Dattani

A Critical Response

edited by
R.K. Dhawan
Tanu Pant

Prestige
an international publishing house

Published by
Prestige Books International
New Delhi 110 060
prestigebooks@gmail.com
Phone: 9818755529

Associate Office
50, Clapham Common Westside
London SW 49 A S, U.K.

Associate Office
P.O. Box 2250, Sydney 2001

Edition 2018
ISBN: 81-7551-160-6

Printed in India

Contents

The Plays of Mahesh Dattani: A Critical Response

R.K. DHAWAN
S.B.S. College, University of Delhi

Mahesh Dattani is the foremost Indian English playwright today. He has written significant plays: *Tara*, *On a Muggy Night in Mumbai*, *Where There's a Will*, *Dance Like a Man*, *Bravely Fought the Queen* and *Final Solutions*. He has received the prestigious Sahitya Akademi Award for his contribution to Indian drama. Dattani is also a film director. He has directed the recently-released film *Morning Raga*, after the award-winning film on alternate sexuality *Mango Souffle*.

In an interview "Personal Agenda," published in *Brunch* on March 21, 2004, Dattani says: "The love of my life is drama and I want to write more plays." (26) The most charismatic quality of Dattani's plays is the wide range of themes that he deals with in his writing. He depicts mainly the middle-class Indian life and focuses on modern subjects like homosexuality, gender identity, human relationships and communalism. He gives expression to the longings and aspirations of the middle-class Indians. As John McRae puts it: "Dattani is the voice of India now." (10) In order to fully evaluate the plays of Dattani, it is desirable to assess them with context to the mainstream Indian drama. Hence first thing first. That is, we should briefly trace the evolution of Indian drama—its origin, growth and development through the ages.

II

The dramatic tradition of the ancient Hindus may be said to have been fully formed even before Greek dramas came to their knowledge. It is clear that the Hindus of over 2000 years ago had their own theory of drama and that their dramatic practice avoided both the severe austerity of Greek tragedy and the opulent extravagance of the ancient Chinese drama.

Bharata's *Natyashastra* in Sanskrit elaborately discusses the ancient stagecraft. All aspects of the drama—stage-setting, music, plot-construction, characterization, dialogue and acting—have borne the close critical scrutiny of the author, and a set of rules to guide the conduct of the stage has been elaborately laid down. It analyses searchingly the factors involved in plot, characters and emotions bringing out the far-reaching significance of '*rasa*.'

Sanskrit drama, in its long and checkered history, has throughout conformed to these classical norms prescribed by Bharata. While being loyal to the highest principles of Indian aesthetic, Sanskrit drama mirrored the essential and eternal India much to the profit and delight of the audience. The best Sanskrit drama had been intimately associated with the stir and manifoldness of the life of a cultured class of people. The works of Bhasa, Shudraka, Kalidasa, Harsha, Bhavabhuti, and Vishakhadatta are the products of vigorous creative energy as well as sustained technical excellence.

Bhasa is the oldest known dramatist who might have flourished some time between 500 BC and 50 BC, a period certainly earlier than that of the celebrated grammarian, Panini. Of the thirty-five plays he is said to have written, only thirteen have come to light. Interestingly enough, he has written not only seven-act and ten-act plays but also one-act plays and one-scene plays. Many of these abound in soliloquies, thus blazing a trail for later playwrights. His masterpieces—*Urubhanga*, *Duta-Vakya* and *Karna*—are known for their tragic intensity and dramatic style.

Later playwrights like Kalidasa and Bhavabhuti distinctly bear the imprint of Bhasa's dramatic style. The supreme achievement of Indian drama is undoubtedly in Kalidasa who is often called the Shakespeare of India. Though he does not have the range and variety of Shakespeare, he has given the world a profounder spiritual vision of life. His magnum opus, *Abhijnana Shakuntala*, is said to be the richest and most completely satisfying romantic drama. Bhavabhuti turned out dramatic poems rather than stage plays. His *Mahaviracharita*, *Malatimadhava* and *Uttararamacharita*, reveal the "poet's maturity of mind, a sense of workmanship, an acute understanding of human mind, and some of the deep values of life."[1]

The Sanskrit drama flourished in its glory under the patronage of the court and the aristocracy till the 12th century when the Mohammedan intrusion shifted the Sanskrit stage. The glory of Sanskrit drama became a thing of the past in the period of decline when it was divorced gradually from the stage. Instead of poets, 'pandits' took to playwriting and produced works on the stock epic themes in a conventional way. The decadent drama distanced itself from life in its sophisticated setting, stereotyped characters and artificial diction. Vidyanatha's play, *Prataparudrakalyana*, provides a patent example of the virtual death of the ancient Indian drama.

III

It was only after the British set up their regime in India that the crippled Indian drama received new strength and witnessed a revival. As Krishna Kriplani points out, the modern Indian drama "owed its first flowering to foreign grafting."[2] With the impact of Western civilization on Indian life, a new renaissance dawned on Indian arts including drama. Furthermore, English education gave an impetus and a momentum to the critical study of not only Western drama, but also classical Indian drama. English and Italian dramatic troupes toured India and performed many English plays, mainly Shakespeare's, in cities like Bombay and Madras. The Portuguese brought a form of dance-drama to the West Coast. A Russian music director, Rebedoff, is said to have produced the first modern drama in Calcutta towards the end of the 18th century. Thus, the Western impact awakened "the dormant, critical impulse in the country to bring Indians face to face with new forms of life and literature, and to open the way for a fruitful cross-fertilization of ideas and forms of expression."[3]

The newly awakened creative efforts first took the form of translations and adaptations from Sanskrit and English drama. Kalidasa's *Shakuntala* was translated into quite a few regional languages. *Mrichchakatika* was translated into Maithili by Ishanatha Jha and *Ratnavali* into Sindhi by Dewan Kauromal. Shakespeare was naturally the most sought after, and among his plays the frequently translated or adopted were *Comedy of Errors*, *The Merchant of Venice*, *Hamlet*, *Othello* and *Cymbeline*. To cite but a few examples, Viresalingam Pantulu's rendering of *All's Well That Ends Well* came out in 1897, a Tamil adaptation of *Cymbeline* in 1898, and a Bengali edition of Shakespeare's plays in four volumes was issued between 1896 and 1902. K.S. Ramaswami Sastri translated *A Midsummer Night's Dream* into Sanskrit. Apart from Shakespeare's plays, Goldsmith's *She Stoops to Conquer* was a favourite play among Indian translators.

The Western impact also quickened the drying roots of Indian native tradition with the sap of a new life, thereby opening the exciting chapter of modern Indian drama written originally in the vernaculars, and at times, translated into English. By the end of the 19th century, there were pioneering efforts boldly employing the mother tongue for creative dramatic expression. The earlier dramatists from different regions of the country tried their hand at different forms—romance, opera, comedy, farce, tragedy, melodrama, and historical play. As a result, the modern Indian drama was a product and blend of many models and forces. When old puranic themes were handled, various approaches—the reformist, the revivalist, the idealistic, the iconoclastic, the frivolous and the allegorical—were tried. Just to mention the most representative plays written in regional languages, we have Khadilkar's mythological play *Keechaka Vadha* in Marathi, Lakshminath Bezbarua and Gohain Barua's historical play *Jaymati* in Assamese, Amanat's opera *Inder Sabha* in Hindi, Ram Shankar Ray's *Kanchi-Kaveri* in Oriya, Gurajada Apparao's social play *Kanyasulkam* in Telugu, T.P. Kailasam's *Tollu-Gatti* in

Kannada, Sundaram Pillai's poetic drama *Manonmaniyam* in Tamil and Tagore's symbolic poetic plays like *Chitra*, *Sacrifice*, *Mukta Dhara*, *Red Oleanders*, and *The Post Office* in Bengali now quite familiar to us in English renderings. Thus, by 1920 in almost all the Indian languages a new drama was thriving, reflecting potent influences of Marxism, psychoanalysis, and the symbolist and surrealist movements.

IV

Although the pre-Independence Indian English drama is notable for its poetic excellence, thematic variety, technical virtuosity, symbolic significance and its commitment to human and moral values, it was by and large not geared for actual stage production. Very few Indian dramatists so far had shown great interest in producing drama for the stage. One singular exception to this phenomenon was Asif Currimbhoy who is rightly hailed as "India's first authentic voice in the theatre."[4] His plays are essentially pieces of theatre. By fusing the elements of pantomime, dance, and song, he succeeds brilliantly in creating powerful auditory and visual images that go a long way in making his plays vitally theatrical.

Currimbhoy is a playwright with a social purpose. He is a prolific dramatist who has thirty plays to his credit dealing with the social, political and religious problems of contemporary society. In a Currimbhoy play, one can discern a definite philosophical basis that can be recognized in the very titles of his plays—*The Hungry Ones*, *The Captives*, *The Doldrummers*, *An Experiment with Truth*, *Goa*, *This Alien . . . Native Land*, and *Om Mane Padma Hun!* The variety of his themes and techniques, the topicality of several of his plays, the social realism and implicit philosophy of his plays, the opulence of his scenes, situations and characters, the bold experimentation in technique, the resourceful improvisation of his stagecraft, and the mastery of his dialogue are some of the qualities that reveal Currimbhoy's dramatic genius. Though in his later plays, Currimbhoy subjects his dramatic art to a strain it cannot bear, his plays remain 'colourful instruments of an intense theatricality.'

V

Quite a few contemporary playwrights have made a significant contribution to the development of Indian English drama. The foremost among them is Nissim Ezekiel, a well-established Indian English poet, who has also enriched Indian English drama in his own characteristic way. His *Three Plays* (1969) consisting of *Nalini, A Marriage Poem* and *The Sleep-Walkers*, and another play, *Song of Deprivation*, expose the hollowness of the urban middle-class life, fickleness of modern lovers, greedy fascination for American life and the hypocrisy and inhibitive nature of contemporary Indian society respectively. Ezekiel is an excellent craftsman. His plays are fine examples of symmetric construction, abounding in irony, wit and humour. They reveal his sharp observation of the oddities in human life and behaviour, providing glimpses of a cross-section of contemporary society. Though they do not meet the full requirements of the stage, they "make pleasant reading" and are known for their "stage-worthiness."[5] And, in the words of Chetan Karnani, "in his satire of current fashion, in his exposure of pose and pretence, Ezekiel comes very close to the spirit of some English social satirists in the theatre."[6]

Some playwrights like Lakhan Deb and Gurcharan Das have made a significant contribution to the development of historical play. Lakhan Deb's *Tiger's Claw* (1947) is a powerful dramatization of Shivaji's killing of Afzal Khan bringing out the heroic nature and nobility of Shivaji. His *Murder at the Prayer Meeting* (1976) deals with the murder of Mahatma Gandhi echoing T.S. Eliot's *Murder in the Cathedral*. Modelled on the technique of Greek tragedy, the play deftly employs the dramatic unities of time, place and action as well as the classical devices of prologue and chorus. Gurcharan Das's *Larins Sahib* (1970) is based on the events in Punjab during 1846-47, and is reconstructed from the documents and letters exchanged by the principal characters. It is a remarkable achievement in historical drama in that the playwright has not only recreated history faithfully, but also suitably captured the essential traits of the historical characters. What is more, he succeeds admirably in evoking the nineteenth century colonial Indian background.

Gieve Patel and Partap Sharma are two other contemporary dramatists who have distinguished themselves. Gieve Patel's *Princes* (1970) is the first Parsi play, set in the semi-urban Parsi sub-culture of the Sanjan-Nargol area of South Gujarat, focusing on two Parsi families and their savage conflict for the possession of a sole male child. It is significant for its experiments with language and its brilliant success in handling situation, character and dialogue. It creates a situation—the obsession with male children—that most Indians can identify with, and creates a language of sub-cultures that characters can speak without straining our credulity. Patel succeeds in evolving "a form of modified English which is not standard English, which has distinctively Indian rhythms; but none of the 'cuteness' or self-conscious phony "Indianness" of other experiments in this genre."[7]

Partap Sharma has carved out a niche for himself among contemporary playwrights by handling the theme of sex in his two plays—*The Professor Has a Warcry* (1970) and *A Touch of Brightness* (1970). The first play brings out the mental anguish of Virendra who becomes aware of his illegitimacy and the second is a realistic portrayal of the red light area in Bombay. Both the plays have been commended for their thematic boldness, character delineation and technical triumph.

VI

In spite of the impressive record of Indian English drama, it has to be conceded that in terms of both quantity and quality, it lags far behind Indian English poetry and particularly Indian English novel. Various reasons have been attributed to the paucity of Indian drama in English. It is generally felt that Indian playwrights in English have failed to draw upon the rich and varied Indian dramatic traditions, as also to make creative use of the rich fund of Indian myth and Indian historical heritage. Yet another important reason given for stunted growth of Indian drama in English is its unsuitability for production on the stage. No doubt, we have had highly talented and enterprising Indians who seriously attempted drama in English, but "seldom for actual stage production."[8] Indian English drama has also suffered for want of a real theatre and a live audience in India. As M.K. Naik puts it, "a play, in order to communicate fully and become a living dramatic experience, needs a real theatre and a live audience. . . . It is precisely the lack of these essentials that has hamstrung Indian drama in English all along."[9]

Above all, the major hurdle for the flourishing of Indian English drama is said to be the lack of a viable language as suitable medium for its expression. It is generally believed that we have very few actable plays mainly because a dialogue between Indians may not sound convincing except when the characters are drawn from an urban, sophisticated milieu. But it is not proper to take such a narrow and shortsighted view of the problem. Rightly approached, this much-dreaded difficulty is more apparent than real. For, confronted by a similar problem in fiction, Raja Rao could solve it by infusing the tempo of Indian life into his English expression. Similarly, "when Shakespeare makes his Romans speak in Elizabethan English, we do not bat an eyelid; when Shaw's St. Joan speaks English, no one asks whether the French girl held a certificate of proficiency in that language; and when Brecht makes the good Woman of Setzuan express herself in German, we are not horrified."[10] "The truth is that the spectators are always in their senses, and know from the first Act to the last, that the stage is only a stage and that the players players."[11] Therefore the Indian English playwrights need not have any qualms about making their Indian characters speak in English. If they can take sufficient care to create convincing characters in live situations, perhaps, the language would take care of itself.

On top of that, the Indian English dramatists should strive hard to turn their professional and natural limitations into artistic assets in the manner of their ancient forebears. They can, however, do so only if they succeed in overcoming the temptation to play to a foreign gallery and to blindly imitate the Western models. They must necessarily write with a sense of rootedness revealing a true Indian sensibility. However, they should be grounded in contemporary problems while deriving inspiration and sustenance from their ancient culture. While drawing on Indian history epics, legends, myths, folklore art and culture, they should not lose sight of the innovative themes and techniques and current trends in the world drama today. Given these conditions, and given a living theatre and a live audience, there is no reason why Indian drama in English should lag behind Indian English poetry and fiction any longer, that too in a country in which drama was hailed as the "Fifth Veda," and cherished as "Kavyesu naatakam ramyam."

VII

Contemporary Indian drama in English translation has made bold innovations and fruitful experiments in terms of both thematic concerns and technical virtuosities. It has been increasingly turning to history, legend, myth and folklore, tapping their springs of vitality and vocal cords of popularity with splendid results. Mohan Rakesh, Badal Sircar, Vijay Tendulkar and Girish Karnad have remained the most representative of the contemporary Indian drama not only in Hindi, Bengali, Marathi and Kannada respectively but also on the pan-Indian level.

Greatly influenced by Marxism, Mohan Rakesh waged a relentless fight against the traditional stranglehold of Hindi drama, and always endeavoured to project something new and challenging. As Nirad Chaudhuri points out, "With Mohan Rakesh Hindi drama makes a departure from pseudo-modernism and traditional symbolism to the drama of 'non-communication'—the modern man's failure to understand himself or to understand the other person and their mutual failure to understand each other, which is the real tragedy of modern life."[12] His plays dramatize the sufferings of men and women who fall victims to socio-economic hierarchy and cultural hegemony. Particularly, in his plays like *One Day in Ashadha* and *The Great Swans of the Waves*, Rakesh makes use of history and legend to throw light on the contemporary problems. His dialogues have a smooth flow, a meaningful depth, and elemental naturalness suitable to his characters.

While Rakesh uses historical characters to project the breakdown of communication in contemporary life, Badal Sircar uses contemporary situations to project the existential attitude of modern life. Popularly known as a 'barefoot playwright,' Badal Sircar stands in the forefront of a new theatrical movement in India. He has created a genuine people's theatre, known as Third Theatre, a theatre supported and created by the people, and not merely performed by the people. Transcending the limits and limitations of the traditional and folk theatres, the Third Theatre is "a composite of a four way flow of influences—actor to actor, audience to actor, actor to audience and audience to audience."[13] It is essentially a flexible, portable and inexpensive Theatre, aiming at not simply enlightening the people on socio-economic and political problems, but leading them to constructive action with a view to bringing about a social change.

Sircar's later plays, *Procession, Bhoma* and *Stale News*, are based on the concept of the Third Theatre. *Procession* is certainly the most popular of the three plays. It is about the search for "a real home"—a new society based on equality. The chief concern of the play is to show "real way" to a new society in which man does not have to live by exploiting man, and in which each works according to his/her ability and gets according to his/her needs. The leitmotif of the play is symbolized in the characters of Old Man and Khoka who represent the old and new generations as well as the past and the present. *Bhoma* is a dramatization of life of the oppressed peasants in rural India through a series of scenes in which he is socially and economically exploited. *Stale News* deals with the theme of revolt, centring round a young man who is bombarded with biting bits of information full of contradictions and contrasts which come to him as stale news.

Leading the vanguard of the avant-garde Marathi Theatre, Vijay Tendulkar symbolizes the new awareness and attempts of Indian dramatists of the last quarter of the century, to depict the agonies, suffocations and cries of man, focusing on the middle-class society. In all his plays, he harps upon the theme of isolation of the individual and his confrontation with the hostile surroundings. Influenced by Artaud, Tendulkar relates the problem of anguish to the theme of violence in most of his plays. He does not consider the occurrence of human violence as something loathsome or disgusting inasmuch as it is innate in human nature. He says: "unlike the communists I don't think violence can be eliminated in a classless society, or, for that matter, in any society. The spirit of aggression is something that human being is born with. Not that it is bad. Without violence man might have turned into a vegetable."[14] While depicting violence on the stage, Tendulkar does not dress it up with any fancy trapping so as to make it palatable but rather keeps it raw and natural.

Small wonder then, if Tendulkar's plays like *Sakharam Binder*, *Ghashiram Kotwal*, *Silence! The Court is in Session* created a storm in society. Tendulkar raises several questions about love, sex, marriage and moral values prevalent in Indian society, making ample use of irony, satire, pathos and mock-element to highlight the hollowness of middle-class morality. He exposes the hypocrisy in the traditional Indian society. In his latest plays, *To Hell with Destiny* and *The Tour*, Tendulkar highlights the typical middle-class mentality and value system. In both the plays, Tendulkar economizes on the number and range of characters, situations and episodes, giving wider scope to deeper interpretations and meaningful corollaries.

Vijay Tendulkar's plays, along with those of playwrights like Girish Karnad, Badal Sircar and Mohan Rakesh, have changed the face of Indian theatre. Tendulkar was born in a Brahmin family on 7 January 1928. He wrote his first play while still in school and later worked as an apprentice in a bookshop. He took up journalism and was an assistant editor of Marathi dailies like *Navbharat*, *Maratha* and *Loksatta*. Tendulkar has written plays, short stories, features and television serials in Hindi. Recipient of many prestigious awards like Kamladevi Chattopadhyaya award, Sangeet Natak Akademi award and Kalidas Samman award, he is fighter for cultural freedom, the freedom which is stifled at present by various forces.

Tendulkar has changed the form and pattern of Indian drama by demolishing the three-act play and creating new models. By developing the flexible as well as carefully crafted forms, modes of recitation and story telling specific to his region, he has managed to bridge the gulf between traditional and modern theatre by creating a vibrant new theatrical form, an example of which is the play *Ghashiram Kotwal*.

Unlike Badal Sircar and Vijay Tendulkar who delve into the problems of middle-class society, Girish Karnad, the well-known Kannada playwright, goes back to myths and legends with a view to making them a vehicle of a new vision. By exploiting the various myths, he shows the absurdity of modern life with all its elemental passions and conflicts, and man's eternal struggle to achieve perfection. In his plays, *Yayati, Tughlaq, Hayavadana, Tale Danda* and *Naga-Mandala*, he tries to evolve a symbolic form out of a tension between the archetypal and mythic experience and to a living response to life and its values in his attempt to give new meanings to the past from the vantage point of the present. In the reworking of myths creatively, Karnad reminds us of T.P. Kailasam and Rangacharya. He has admirably succeeded in his attempt to show the Indian playwright as well as to the world theatre community at large how our past and present can coalesce to give present-day existence meaning and to theatre activity a direction. Thus, the contemporary India drama in English translation has achieved a thorough synthesis of the three traditions—classical, folk and Western—which lead to the discovery of a new form as well as a new style of production.

Girish Karnad has given the Indian theatre a richness that could probably be equated only with his talents as an actor-director. His contribution goes beyond theatre: he has directed feature films, documentaries and television serials. He has represented India in foreign lands as an emissary of art and culture.

VIII

Very recently Indian English drama has shot into prominence. Younger writers like Mahesh Dattani and Manjula Padmanabhan have infused new life into this branch of writing. The thirty-eight-year-old Bangalore-based Dattani has published forceful plays like *Where There is a Will*, *Final Solutions* and *Tara*. Padmanabhan's Onassis award-winning *Harvest* has achieved worldwide acclaim. Incidentally, both Dattani and Padmanabhan do not write on the traditional subjects. Dattani writes about mean, ugly, unhappy things of life; Padmanabhan projects a dehumanized, terrifying world in which mothers sell their sons for the price of rice. Her play *Harvest* is about an impoverished family living in a single room in a chawl of Bombay. Population explosion has rendered the city dwellers into helpless, poor, dehumanized lot struggling for their survival. In this scenario, driven by hunger and unemployment, twenty-year-old Om Prakash decides to become an organ donor and mortgages his body to a white First World buyer. Padmanabhan projects in her play a more serious, grim and unpalatable world than Dattani. But her play is rather intellectual and not suited for stage, unlike the plays of Dattani which have been quite successful on the stage and have captured the imagination of the middle-class audience.

IX

Dattani's plays are written for the stage. As poetry is meant to be read in order to enjoy, the plays are meant to be staged. It is the visual quality and dramatic effect which are of paramount importance. Dattani accordingly suits his material to the space, reshaping and fine-tuning his texts constantly.

Dattani's plays have a universal appeal. They can be staged anywhere in the world; they would draw full attention of the audience. Dattani moulds his subject in such a way that it is both topical as also has a wider appeal. His plays speak across linguistic and cultural barriers. It may however be noted that these plays are essentially rooted in the Indian settings. Dattani makes an abundant use of Indian mythology, rituals and traditions and contemporary problems India is beset with, but he elevates these themes to higher level, touching the human chords that emanate love, happiness, sexual fulfillment and the problem of identity. Though he lives in Karnataka, he writes about the whole nation of India, about the whole world he lives in. More than that, he is able to merge the past and the present as well as geographical locations. It is in the fitness of things that we must make an attempt at evaluating the playwright's thematic concerns as well as his exploration of, and experimentation with stage.

The plays of Mahesh Dattani emerged as 'fresh arrival' in the domain of Indian English drama in the last decade of the twentieth century. The plays have a great 'contemporary' value. "They are plays of today," writes John McRae in his introduction to Dattani's plays, "sometimes as actual as to cause controversy, but at the same time they are plays which embody many of the classic concerns of world drama." (7) The most significant contribution of Dattani is perhaps his use of language. Dattani uses in his plays the kind of English as spoken by people in India.

It has been appropriately said that the starting point of many of the greatest plays in history is the family. This idea has been so with the Indian drama as also with European drama. Like Mohan Rakesh, Dattani takes the family unit as the locale of his plays. Human relationships and the family unit have indeed been at the heart of Dattani's representation.

NOTES

1. G.K. Bhat, *Bhavabhuti* (New Delhi: Sahitya Akademi, 1979), p. 34.
2. Krishna Kriplani, *Literature of Modern India* (New Delhi: National Book Trust, 1982), p. 40.
3. K.R. Srinivasa Iyengar, *Drama in Modern India*, p. 4.
4. Faubion Bowers, "Introduction," *Asif Currimbhoy's Plays* (New Delhi: Oxford & IBH, n.d.), p. xii.
5. Prema Nandakumar, "Indians Writing in English Three Cheers," *Indian Literature*, Vol. XIII, No. 4 (December, 1970), p. 36.
6. Chetan Karnani, *Nissim Ezekiel* (New Delhi: Arnold-Heinemann, 1974), p. 126.
7. Eunice De Souza, "Some Recent Plays in English," *Perspectives on Indian Drama in English*, p. 163.
8. K.R. Srinivasa Iyengar, *Indian Writing in English*, p. 226.

9. M.K. Naik, "The Achievement of Indian Drama in English," *Perspectives on Indian Drama in English*, p. 181.
10. *Ibid.*, p.191.
11. Samuel Johnson, "Preface to Shakespeare," Walter Raleigh, *Johnson on Shakespeare* (London: 1940), p. 27.
12. Badal Sircar, *Changing Language of Theatre at the Present Time* (New Delhi: ICCR, 1982), pp. 25-26.
13. Interview, *India Today*, December 16-31, 1985, p. 157.
14. "Hindi Drama," *Comparative Indian Literature*, ed. K.M. George Madras: Macmillan India, 1984), pp. 512-13.

Mahesh Dattani: The Face of Indian Drama

TANU PANT
University of Lucknow

Mahesh Dattani, one of the exponents of modern Indian drama, is a renowned playwright and an active theatre practitioner. He is responsible for successfully launching the Indian theatre in English. He has carved a niche for himself not only in India but also in the West with his British production of *Bravely Fought the Queen* under the aegis of Michael Walling's Border Crossings.

It is not always a story and a tale that Mahesh Dattani wants to tell his audiences across the world. It is sometimes a cause, a point of view, a sense of contemporaneity and a social message too. The various plays that he has written deal with some issues prevalent in the society and exposes it most honestly and candidly. His plays like *Bravely Fought the Queen*, *On a Muggy Night in Mumbai*, *Tara*, *Final Solutions*, *Thirty Days of September*, etc. deal with various issues like homosexuality, gender discrimination, communalism and child sexual abuse.

It was after much deliberation that I came to a conclusion to undertake a study of his two most challenging plays, *Tara*, and *Bravely Fought the Queen* which deal with the issue of gender discrimination, women exploitation and homosexuality. In this way I will not only evince his dramatic traditions but also trace his evolutions as a dramatist. I will first deal with the origin of Indian drama leading to the establishment of modern Indian drama and theatre as well and finally placing the position of Mahesh Dattani in the present scenario and liw contribution to the modern Indian drama and theatre as well by discussing the two most popular plays written by him, *Tara* and *Bravely Fought the Queen*.

In order to explore everything about the Indian drama and theatre and also to reveal the achievements of Mahesh Dattani the present project has been divided into the following sections. Section 1, "Origin of Indian Drama," deals with the beginnings of Indian drama from the ancient times to the present day. It gives information about the origin of the *Natyashastra* and the changes brought about in the Indian theatrical art. Section 2, "Mahesh Dattani: The Face of Modern Indian Drama," gives a brief introduction of Mahesh Dattani as a playwright and as a theatre practitioner and examines his works dealing with contemporary social issues like sexuality, gender discrimination and communalism. It also deals with the achievements of Mahesh Dattani as a playwright. Section 3 discusses the play *Tara* and aims at exploring the gender discrimination prevalent in urban educated middle-class families living in metropolitan cities like Bangalore, Mumbai, etc. Section 4 discusses the play *Bravely Fought the Queen* and aims at exploring the issue of women exploitation and homosexuality prevalent in the urban families living in a metropolitan city like Bangalore. Conclusion sums up the argument making a general assessment of Mahesh Dattani as a playwright and points out certain similarities between him and Shaw, Ibsen and Shakespeare.

Origin of Indian Drama

India has the longest and the richest tradition in Drama. Origin of Indian Drama can be traced to the ancient rituals and seasonal festivities of the Vedic Aryans. The dramatic performances of those times mainly included depiction of events of daily life accompanied by music. Some members of the tribe acted as if they were wild animals and some others were the hunters. Those who acted as animals like goats, buffaloes, reindeers and monkeys were chased by those playing the role of hunters and a mock hunt was enacted.

In such a crude and a simple way was drama performed during the age of the Vedic Aryans. Later, different episodes from the *Ramayana*, the *Mahabharata* and the *Bhagvadgita* were picked up and enacted out in front of the people. This kind of [illegible]a performance is still very popular in India especially during the time of Dussehra when the episode of the killing of Ravana is enacted out in different parts of the country.

There are references to drama in Patanjali's *Vyakarna Mahabhashya*, Jain's *Aagam of Raypaseni Sutta* as well as Vatsyayan's *Kamasutra*, Kautilya's *Arthasastra* and Panini's *Ashtabhyan.* Thus the origin of Sanskrit Drama dates back to 1000 B.C

Bharata's *Natyasastra* is the most significant work on Indian dance and drama. Besides everything about composition, production, and enjoyment of ancient drama, a wealth of information of types of drama, dress, stage equipment, production and music is also dealt with in detail. According to the legend, when the world passed from the golden age to the silver age, and people became addicted to sensual pleasures and jealousy, anger, desire and greed filled their hearts. The world was then inhabited by gods, demons, yakshas, rakshasas, nagas and gandharvas. It was the gods among them who, led by Lord Indra, approached god Brahma and requested him thus:

> Please give us something which would not only teech us but be pleasing both to eyes and ears.[1]

The Creator nodded graciously; and fell into a profound meditation and out of the divine thought sprang the *Natya Veda*, that is the veda of the theatre. Such was the will of the Lord who made the fifth Veda, drawing the quintessence of drama out of the four Vedas, dance from the *Rig Veda*, song from the *Sama Veda*, mimicry from *Yajur Veda* and passion from *Atharva Veda*. Brahma then summoned Vishwakarma, Celestial Architect, that he might build a stage in Indra's heaven. The sage Bharata was appointed as theatrical manager and as conductor of the heavenly performances. Bharata is thus regarded as the deity of the Indian theatre.

Bharata ascribed a divine origin to drama and considered it as the fifth Veda. Its origin seems to be from religious dancing. According to Bharata, poetry (kavya), dance (nritta), and mime (nritya) in life's play (lila) produce emotion (bhava) but only drama (natya) produces flavour (rasa). The drama uses the eight basic emotions of love, joy (humour), anger, sadness, pride, fear, aversion and wonder attempting to resolve them in the ninth holistic feeling of peace. Thus, when the dramatic art was well comprehended, the *Natyaveda* was performed on the occasion of the celebration of Lord Indra's victory over the asuras and danavas. In the *Natyashastra* there is a verse in its sixth chapter which can be quoted as Bharat Muni's own summary of his dramatic theory: "The combination called natya is a mixture of rasa, bhavas, abhinayas, dharmis, vrittis, pravrittis, siddhi, svaras, instruments, song and theatre-house."[2]

The most renowned and talented dramatists of the ancient era are Ashwaghosha, Bhasa, Shudraka, Kalidasa, Harsha, Bhavabhuti, Vishakhadatta, Bhattanarayana, Murari and Rajashekhara who enriched Indian theatre with their works like *Madhyamavyaayoda*, *Urubhangam*, *Karnabharan*, *Mrichkatikam*, *Abhigyana Shakuntalam*, *Malavikagnimitram*, *Uttar Ramacharitam*, *Mudrarakshasa*, *Bhagavadajjukam*, *mattavilasa* etc.

The *Natyashastra* legend indicates an intimate relation between the idea of dancing and dramatic representation. Dance has an important role in the birth of the Indian theatre. As dance is a function of life, even from the primitive to the most cultured community, drama finds a semi-religious origin from the art of dancing.

The theatrical practice of India is a fine example of Hieropraxis (sacred action). The chief characteristics of hieropraxis drama may be stated briefly:

i There was no primacy of the aural, particularly of the speech content, over the visual content.

ii The visual was never intended to be realistically representational but evolved instead as a sign language.

iii All gesture and body movement was highly embellished and codified and was mimetic of the cultural semiones and habitual gestures of the people it represented.

iv A major part of hieropraxis was dance. It was often included as an act of worship besides being a dramatic representation.

v Simple speech was used in a limited way but stylish speech, declamation and song dialogue were amply used.

vi The visual and the aural were combined into a unified whole to produce a theatrical reality which was not meant to reflect directly upon the world beyond theatre but was designed to be absorbing in itself. It was also meant to produce an elevated state of feeling in the audience.

Literally 'Abhinaya' means nothing more than communication. Abhi (specially) naya (providmng), the meaning from the actor to the audience is Abhinaya. Bharat Muni postulated four kinds of Abhinayas and they are characterized as (a) Angika, pertaining to the movement of head, torso and limbs, (b) Vachika, consisting of speech, (c) Sattvika, expressive of deep emotions indicated by subtle facial changes, (d) Aharya, related to the use of costumes.

The body (angika) abhinaya can aim at communicating by concentrating on one of the three ways: by body stances (sariraja), by facial expressions (mukhaja), or by movements (cestakrta). The human figure is divided into six major and minor body parts. Head, hands, breast, sides, hips, and legs are the major parts and eyes, brows, nose, lips, cheeks and chin are the minor ones. For each of these body parts, different movements are prescribed in the *Natyashastra*. The Vachika Abhinaya is synonymous with the use of svara, language as inflected dramatic dialogue. The speech or verbal (vachika) acting is the prime medium of communication. The Sattvika bhavas in the theatre are to be enacted as Anukarna of general behaviour. Preparations made in the green room are called Aharya, i.e. the actor's costume and the stage props.

Till the fifteenth century, plays of Sanskrit tradition were performed on stage in Tamil Nadu, Kerala, Karnataka, Andhra, Uttar Pradesh, and Gujarat. Sanskrit dramas were staged approximately upto the fifteenth century, but thereafter, Indian drama activity almost ceased due to foreign invasions on India.

The beginnings of Loknatya (People's Theatre) are noticed in every state of India from the seventeenth century onwards. We see in Bengal "Yatrakirtaniya," "Paal" and "Gaan"; in Madhya Pradesh "Mach"; in Kashmir "Bhandya Thar" and in Gujarat the forms were "Bhavai" and "Ramleela"; in Northern India there were "Nautanki," "Bhand," "Ramleela" and "Rasleela"; in Maharashtra "Tamasha"; in Rajasthan "Raas" and "Jhoomer"; in Punjab "Bhangra" and "Song"; while in Assam it was "Ahiya-nat" and "Ankinatya"; in Bihar it was "Videshiya"; and "Chhau" in West Bengal and Bihar. The distinguishing feature of this dance drama is the skilful use of masks and costumes supplemented by the right tempo of music. The chhau dancers worship Lord Shiva and Goddess Parvati. It is performed in open air on a raised platform. The people living in Southern India began presenting the plays in their temples (Devasthanas) in their ancient traditional forms with accompaniment of music and dance called "Bhavvatmela," "Yakshgan" and "Kudiyattam."

The rise of the modern Indian drama dates back to the eighteenth century when the British Empire consolidated its stable power in India. In 1765 one Russian drama lover Horasin Lebedef and Bengali drama lover Gulokhnath had staged two English comedies *Disgaij* and *Love is the Best Doctor*. But the real beginning was in 1831 when Prasanna Kumar Thakur established "Hindu Rangmanch" at Calcutta and staged Wilson's English translation of Bhavabhuti's Sanskrit drama *Uttar Ramacharitam*. Social drama of Girish Chanda Ghosh, historical dramas of D.L. Roy and artistic dramas of Rabindranath Tagore (*Mukta-Dhara*, *Chandalika*) continued to reach upto the stage of realistic dramas during the period of the worst-ever famines of Bengal and the Second World War. This was the beginning of the Parallel Theatre.

Modern or Parallel Theatre is a more realistic reflection of the existing Indian environment. Performed in a host of regional languages, Parallel Theatre is performed in several styles and techniques.

Closely following the trends of Bengali theatre, theatres of Marathi, Kannada, Gujarati, Oriya and Hindi were also developing. Vishnu Das Bhave was a pioneer in Marathi who wrote and staged *Sita Swayambar* in 1843. His first Hindi drama *Raja*

Gopichand became very famous and it resulted in the formation of many professional groups such as Kirloskar Natak Mandali of Anna Sahib Kirloskar. Vijay Tendulkar gave a new dimension to the Indian theatre with his effective plays like *Ghashiram Kotwal, Silence! The Court is in Session*, *Kamala*, and several other plays which contamn a subtle critique of modern Indian society, and a distinct character and message. Mahesh Elkunchwar defines the modernist, with reference to Tendulkar's plays, as one "who really confronts the problems of his time and accepts the challenges of his subject material."[3]

Khanolkar, V.V. Shirwadkar (*Doorche Dive*, *Natsamrat*), Satish Alekar (*Mahanirvan* [1974], *Begum Barve* [1979]), Jayavant Dalvi and Govind Deshpande carried on this tradition. In the middle of the nineteenth century Indian theatre was equally influenced by the Western literature and the feelings of nationalism and pride in the glorious past of the country. As Harish Trivedi points out in his book *Colonial Transactions*: "Since the introduction of English literature in India in 1835, . . . the influence on Indian writers of English education . . . have been by far the strongest influences . . . from Shakespeare to T.S. Eliot were received and processed by us (Indians) in about six decades."[4]

Mahesh Elkunchwar while discussing the importance of the influence of western literature on Indian theatre says: "the liberalism, the catholicity of taste, the spirit of frank enquiry into human life, a stress on individuality rather than on a system of accepted social and moral values: all these are gifts to us given by the west."[5]

In 1852-1853, the famous Parsi Theatre was launched in Bombay which influenced the whole country in no time. Postaji Pharmji was the pioneer in establishing the Parsi theatre company in India. Many new theatre experiences were brought up on stage during Parsi theatre's evolution in India. On the other hand, the amateur theatre also developed with the works of Bharatendu Harishchandra, acclaimed as the Father of Hindi Drama.

Indian theatre and drama got a new footing when Kendriya Sangeet Natak Akademi was started in January 1953. Institutions like Anamika in Calcutta (1955), Theatre Unit in Bombay (1954) and Three Arts Club (1948), Little Theatre Group (1951), Independence Theatre (1959) also played a great role in establishing the modern Indian theatre. State academies were also set up in most of the states in 1950s.

However, the most important development was the starting of the National School of Drama at New Delhi. Set up by the Sangeet Natak Akademi in 1959, it became an independent entity, fully financed by the government in 1975.

In the 1960s by suitable mixing of various styles and techniques from Sanskrit, medieval folk and Western theatre, the modern Indian theatre was given a new, versatile and broader approach at every level of creativity. Slowly, many writers broke the barriers of regional languages and produced many good works at national level. Badal Sircar, Girish Karnad (*Hayavadana* [1975], *Nagamandala* [1990]), Vijay Tendulkar, Mohan Rakesh (*Aadhe-Adhure*, *Aashaad ka Ek Din*), Adya Rangacharya and Dharamveer Bharati (*Swarg aur Prithvi*, *Saans ki Kalam se*) are the few among them. Badal Sircar is one of the major playwrights of modern India, one of the makers of modern Indian theatre. "The Third Gaze: The Theatre of Badal Sircar," was once described by Rustom Bharucha "as the most rigorously non-commercial political theatre in India."[6]

Sircar wrote between 1963-1970. His is a world of everyday reality well shown in his plays like *Evam Indrajit* (1963), the most successful of his plays, *Pagla Ghora* (1967), *Baki Itihaas* (1965), *Tringsha Shatabdi* (1966) etc.

The year 1972 was a landmark year for Indian vernacular theatre, Vijay Tendulkar's Marathi play *Ghashiram Kotwal* made waves by its brilliant use of "Tamasha" folk form of Maharashtra in modern contemporary theatre. This led to the birth of a new breed of directors like B.V. Karanth, Habib Tanveer, Bansi Kaul and Rattan Thiyyam. Recently 'Dishantar' group of Om Shivpuri and 'Abhiyan' of Rajinder Nath have staged many notable dramas which will be remembered for long. By staging *Agra Bazar*, *Guinea Pig* etc. 'Naya Theatre' of Habib Tanveer has created a new theatrical style and earned a fame at international level.

In recent years the country has also produced talented playwrights who have chosen English as their medium. Some of the Indian English plays like Gurcharan Das's *Mira*, Partap Sharma's *A Touch of Brightness*, and Asif Currimbhoy's *The Dumb Dancer*, have been staged in the west. During the last few years, several plays originally written in the regional languages have been translated into English. Referring to this, Gurcharan Das told R. Parthasarathy some years ago in the course of an interview: "English theatre in India will have to project the kind of hybrid English we speak, interspersed with Indian expressions."[7]

Manjula Padmanabhan was the first Indian to earn international acclaim with her play *Harvest*, a futuristic play that deals with the exploitation of the human body in the 21st century. It won the highest Greek honour. Alienation and marginalisation play a large role in her books. Her other works include *Lights Out* and *Getting There*.

Badal Sircar, Vijay Tendulkar and Girish Karnad have contributed to the modernization of the face of the Indian theatre. Another upcoming talented playwright is Mahesh Dattani who touched upon the sensitive issues of communalism, sexuality both heterosexual and homosexual, religious tension and gender issues, while still focusing on human relationships and personal and moral choices which are the classic concerns of the world of drama. It is a range of emotions that the readers can experience for his plays or films, ranging from *Dance Like a Man*, *Final Solutions*, *Tara*, *Bravely Fought the Queen*, *On a Muggy Night in Mumbai* to *Mango Soufflé* and now ready for release *Morning Raga*.

Dattani, like his predecessors Sircar and Tendulkar, wants to highlight the issues of the contemporary society. Widely varied in thematic and stylistic content, Dattani's plays transformed the face of urban theatre in India.

Mahesh Dattani: The Face of Modern Indian Drama

Mahesh Dattani is arguably one of the best playwrights the country has ever produced. Born in Bangalore on 7 August 1958, Dattani studied in Baldwin's High School and St. Joseph's College of Arts and Science, Bangalore. He is a graduate in History, Economics and Political Science. He is a Postgraduate in Marketing and Advertising Management. He has worked as a copywriter in an advertising firm and subsequently with his father in the family business.

Dattani's theatre group Playpen was formed in 1984 and he has directed several plays for them ranging from classical Greek to contemporary works. The author of more than 15 plays, he made his directorial debut with *Mango Soufflé*.

Over a career spanning twenty-five years he has written radio plays for the BBC and the film script of *Ek Alag Mausam* and has even had two collections of his plays published. The *International Herald Tribune* while praising Mahesh Dattani described him as "One of India's best and most serious contemporary playwrights writing in English."[8]

Even as a child he yearned to be a part of the exciting world of Drama and was impressed by the popular Gujarati plays he saw during his childhood in Bangalore. His own favourite playwrights as a child were Tennessee Williams and Arthur Miller. The other two playwrights who influenced Dattani a great deal are described by himself thus: "The playwright Madhu Rye influenced me a great deal in his portrayal of middle class Gujarati hypocrisies. Vijay Tendulkar's *Silence! The Court is in Session* and *Sakharam Binder* impressed me with their complex portrayal of women characters."[9]

Dattani owes his success to the fact that he had a theatre company which produced his plays and to Alyque Padamsee who spotted his talent, built it up and brought it out into the larger world of theatre in Bombay and subsequently in Delhi, Calcutta and London. Alyque Padamsee says: "At last we have a playwright who gives sixty million English-speaking Indians an identity."[10]

Alyque Padamsee, the giant theatre figure, helped Mahesh Dattani a great deal in building his self-esteem as well as assisted him in securing a regular audience for his plays. As Mahesh Dattani points out in his Preface: "Alyque believed in my work even before I belmeved in it myself. He gave me the courage to call myself a professional playwright and director." (xii)

In 1998, Dattani won the Sahitya Akademi Award for his book of plays *Final Solutions and Other Plays* published by East-West Books, Chennai. The Sahitya Akademi Award citation says: "[Dattani's work] probes tangled attitudes in contemporary India towards communal differences, consumerism and gender . . . a brilliant contribution to Indian drama in English."[11]

Mahesh Dattani is India's first playwright to be awarded the Sahitya Akademi Award for his contribution to the world of drama. His plays deal with religious tension, sexuality and gender issue. Alyque Padamsee calls him one of the "most serious contemporary playwrights."

He is a director, actor, dancer, teacher and writer, all rolled into one. He is a director par excellence and many of his plays have been staged to universal acclaim. He has starred in several well-known plays and has won accolades for his sterling performance in them. Dattani is also an accomplished dancer. His landmark production *Dance Like a Man* featuring a traditional Carnatic musical score and Bharatnatyam won rave reviews in the *New York Times*. Dattani teaches theatre courses at the summer session programme of Portland State University, Oregon, U.S.A., and conducts workshops regularly at his studio and elsewhere. But his international acclaim rests on his writing credentials which include plays like *Where There's a Will*, *Tara*, *Bravely Fought the Queen*, *Final Solutions* and *On a Muggy Night in Mumbai*.

Ever since his first play, *Where There's a Will*, in 1988, he has chronicled the social victim and the follies, foibles and prejudices of Indian society. He has criticized and exposed the Indian middle class in many of his plays including *Where There's a Will* and *In Quiet and Night Life*. Some of his plays are eloquent defences of society's outcasts and would-be rebels, people forced to live double lives in order to satisfy the prying eyes of society. These plays include *On a Muggy Night in Mumbai*, a compassionate look at the life and tensions of a homosexual community tucked away in Mumbai. *Do the Needful*, Dattani's earlier radio play for BBC, also deals with the coming out of homosexuality.

Both *On a Muggy Night in Mumbai* and *Do the Needful* are probably the first Indian plays to boldly deal with the subject of homosexuality. The play *Final Solutions* is about partition and how the engendered suspicion only deepens from generation to generation.

Dattani tackles issues that afflict societies the world over. Just like Ibsen and Shaw, Dattani also exposes the evils prevalent in the society. Dealing with issues like male-female ascendance divide (*Tara*), the patriarchal tradition (*Where There's a Will! Dance Like a Man*), consumerism, communalism, Dattani holds back nothing. He uses the world of comic theatre to encase the bitterness of the truths he is dealing with and like Bernard Shaw, Dattani also wants to use the theatre as a powerful tool for bringing about the necessary social change. Dattani excels in mirroring his society. Mahesh Dattani in an interview says: "Theatre to me is a reflection of what you observe. . . . I write plays for the sheer pleasure of communicating through this dynamic medium."[12]

Dattani, like his predecessors Vijay Tendulkar and Badal Sircar, believes in the fact that a playwright should write about the evils present in the society of his time and present it before the audience. For this purpose Dattani uses the medium of stage to present the problems to the audience as theatre is very close to real life. Dattaṇi here echoes the words of Shakespeare who compared stage to the real life in his play *As You Like It*:

> All the world's a stage,
> And all the men and women merely players:
> They have their exits and their entrances;
> And one man in his time plays many parts.[13]

In his plays, Dattani takes on what he calls the 'invisible issues' of Indian society. By pulling out taboo subjects from under the rug and placing them on stage for public discussion, Dattani challenges the gonstructions of 'India' and 'Indian' as they have traditionally been defined in modern theatre. He encourages other playwrights to do the same: "Our culture is so rich with tradition, and that's a great advantage and a great disadvantage as well, because . . . we're living in the present and there are so many challenges facing us—you just have to cross the road and you have an issue, . . . I think it is very important for our country to spawn new playwrights . . . who reflect honestly and purely our lives, because . . . that is our contribution to the world." (319)

His plays have varied content and varied appeal. His characters struggle for some kind of freedom and happiness under the weight of tradition, cultural constructions of gender, and repressed desire. Marjorie Boulton says: "All drama has to be contemporary in its immediate appeal."[14]

Dattani seems to follow this statement strictly as he writes about issues which are very contemporary in nature like gender issues, homosexuality, lesbianism, communalism and religious issues. His plays depict marginalized groups of society, people who are considered misfits in a society where stereotyped attitudes and notions reign supreme.

Dattani does not indulge in dealing with colonial and post-colonial issues like the writers Shrilal Shukla (*Raag Darbari*) and Phanishwar Nath Renu (*Maila Aanchal*). But what makes him one of India's finest playwrights is the manner in which he speaks to the audience, i.e., straight from the heart. He does not provide ready-made solutions or fully resolved ending. Like Shaw, he presents the flaw before the people and in this way make people aware that such problems are a part of the society and cannot remain veiled for a long time.

In his play *Tara*, he does not provide a solution to the prevalent gender biases in the society but simply removes the veil and exposes it in its most bitter form. Another play of Dattani, *Bravely Fought the Queen* boldly exposes the prevalence of women exploitation and homosexuality which is not a western concept anymore but very much a part of the Indian society too. He aims not at changing society but only seeks to offer some scope for reflection in the hope that his plays will give the audience some kind of insight into their own lives.

Tara

Mahesh Dattani bears life to the bone, dealing with gender issues; he is a spokesperson of all the marginalized people. Every individual, he says, "wants to be part of society, of the mainstream but we must acknowledge that it is a forced harmony."[15]

In his play *Tara*, we find the idea of 'forced harmony' recurring as it does in several other plays he has authored like *Bravely Fought the Queen*, *On a Muggy Night in Mumbai*, etc. *Tara*, written by Dattani in the year 1990, was first performed as *Twinkle Tara* at the Chowdiah Memorial Hall, Bangalore on 23 October 1990 by Playpen Performing Arts Group. It was subsequently performed as *Tara*, at Sophia Bhabha Hall by Theatre Group, Bombay on 9 November 1991. Dattani was also awarded the Sahitya Kala Award for best production, *Tara*, in the year 2000.

Mahesh Dattani's plays are played out on multi-level sets where interior and exterior become one, and geographical locations collapse—in short, his settings are as fragmented as the families who inhabit them.

The play *Tara* is also performed on a multi-level set. The lowest level occupies a major portion of the stage. It represents the house of the Patels. It is seen only in memory and may be kept as stark as possible. The next level represents the bedsitter of the older Chandan (referred to as Dan) in a suburb of London. This is the only realistic level. Behind, on a higher level, is a chair in which Dr. Thakkar remains seated throughout the play.

Tara is a riveting play that questions the role of a society that treats the children of the same womb in two different ways. Dattani's *Tara* is a poignant play about a boy and a girl who are joined together at the hip and have to be separated surgically, an operation which will mean the death of the one of the two. The fact that the injustice perpetrated by the victim's own mother whose preference is to the male child makes the play more powerful suggesting that it is women who continue the chain of injustice. Another very pertinent example of the injustice perpetrated by a mother on her daughter is Shashi Deshpande's *The Dark Holds No Terror* (1980), where Saru's mother does not get reconciled to the birth of a daughter. Saru's birth is accompanied by terrible rain; the mother perhaps sees the birth as a catastrophe. She shows her dislike of Saru openly as compared to her brother Dhruva. Dhruva dies young and the mother constantly wishes Saru dead in his place. Tle mother and daughter are estranged till the end.

Tara is not just the story of the protagonist of the play Tara, but it is the story of every girl child born in the Indian family whether urban or rural. The situation is aggravated if the girl is physically challenged or there is any other physical or mental deformity in her. It is a bitter example of child abuse present in the Indian societies. Every girl child born in an Indian family does suffer some kind of exploitation and if there is a boy child in the family then the exploitation is very much visible as the privileges are consciously or unconsciously provided to the son. Sudhir Kakar makes a very fine point when he says: "in daughterhood, an Indian girl is a sojourn in her own family and with marriage she becomes less a wife than a daughter-in-law. It is only with motherhood that she comes into her own as a woman and she can make a place for herself in the amily, in the community and in her life circle."[16]

The play seems to be inspired by Tennessee Williams' play *The Glass Menagerie*, which is based on Tennessee's real life story. Tennessee's father belonged to a middle class family like Mr. Patel and his mother belonged to an affluent family of the bureaucrats like Mrs. Patel. Just like the Williams, the Patels also quarrelled over this issue. The similarity is most striking when we encounter the fact that in both the situations the mother allows the doctor to perform the surgery which disturbs the life of each and every member of the family. Just like Tennessee,

Chandan too was very much attached to his sister and the greatest misery falls on him than on any other member of the family.

The scene opens in London with Chandan, now a playwright, reminiscing about his childhood days spent with his sister Tara. Tara and Chandan are two sides of the same self rather than two separate entities and that Dan, in trying to write the story of his own childhood, has to write Tara's story. Dan writes Tara's story to rediscover the neglected half of himself, as a means of becoming whole. He says: "I have my memories. . . . But now I want them to come back. To masticate my memories in my mind and spit out the result to the world in anger."[17]

Through a series of flashbacks we get an insight into their early family life. The play revolves around the Siamese twins, Chandan and Tara Patel; an operation to separate the twins at birth, leaves Tara crippled for life. Fighting against the prejudices the society has for the crippled is Tara, the protagonist of the play. Mahesh Dattani mentioned in one of his interviews to Lakshmi Subramanyam: "I see *Tara* as a play about the male self and the female self. The male self being preferred (if one is to subscribe to conventional categories of masculine traits and feminine traits) in all cultures. The play is about the separation of self and the resultant angst." (129)

Chandan the privileged brother wants to turn his anguish into drama on his sister's childhood. Throughout the play we can feel in Tara that she bears some kind of grudge against the society. She seems to have some kind of aversion with the outside world and her world consisted of only her parents and her brother who she was very close to. Tara's attachment to her brother and the internal anguish is expressed in her conversation with her brother, Chandan, when she says: "May be we still are. Like we've always been. Inseparable. The way we started life. Two lives and one body, in one comfortable womb. Till we were forced out . . . and separated." (325)

The play explores besides exposing the typical Indian mindset, which has from time immemorial preferred a boy child to a girl child. It looks at the triumphs and the failures of an Indian family, comprising of a father (Patel), mother (Bharati), and two children (Chandan and Tara) coping with the trauma of disability which is well expressed by Mahesh Dattani in his interview to Lakshmi Subramanyam: "I focus on cultural emphasis on masculinity and how all the characters are at conflict with that. The parents, the grandfather, the neighbour—they are all in that sense in tension with their own sensibilities, as opposed to cultural sensibilities they may have knowingly or unknowingly subscribed to." (129)

It is later revealed that a decision taken by the mother left Tara crippled for life, and it is this guilt that we notice in Mrs. Patel being revealed throughout the play. She seems to compensate this one decision about her daughter through her excessive concern for her. Her sense of regret is so deep that she agrees to donate her kidney to her daughter so that she may survive for a few more years. In a conversation with her son, she tells him: "I plan to give her happiness. I mean to give her all the love and affection which I can give. It's what she . . . deserves. Love can make up for a lot." (349)

As the play progresses, we are introduced to another interesting character Roopa, the inquisitive and garrulous neighbour of the Patels. She brings some humour to the play. For example when she comments on how dissimilar the twins look.

> Roopa: Funny, you don't resemble each other.
> Chandan: Not all twins are peas in pods. . . . Two peas in a pod. That's something we aren't. (336-37)

On hearing this description Roopa bursts out laughing, much to the surprise of the twins and tells them that the imagery of two 'peas in a pod' is hilarious. Bharati imposes her sense of regret on Roopa too when she bribes her to be her daughter's companion. What follows is an interesting conversation between Bharati and Roopa where Mrs. Patel is just ready to do anything for the sake of Tara's happiness: "You can watch whatever you want! Just be my Tara's friend." (341)

Mrs. Patel's internal turmoil is so strong that it often comes out in her relationship with her husband where she is perpetually complaining about something or the other. Mrs. Patel's father's affluence has always been a bone of contention between Mr. Patel and Mrs. Patel. We see Mrs. Patel constantly complaining to her children about their father and especially about his attitude to their grandfather: "Your father doesn't want us to use them. He doesn't want us to use any of your grandfather's things." (325)

Mr. Patel bears the grudge that Mrs. Patel had always used her father's wealth as a strength against him, and it was this strength that Mrs. Patel used in taking the decision about the separation of the two Siamese twins who were conjoined from the breastbone down through the pelvic region. The surgery was carried out by Dr. Thakkar at the Queen Victoria Memorial Hospital in Bombay. The parents were warned of the odds against survival and in almost all the cases of such kind, one of the twins has always died by the age of four.

Dattani writes plays to be seen and heard, not literature to be read. Hence the play *Tara* has two-fold purpose, first to expose the modern educated urban family's adherence to the conventional attitude of favouring anything that is masculine. The second purpose is to expose the corruption prevalent in the bureaucratic society and the ethical deterioration of the medical profession. This has been very well described by Mr. Patel in his conversation with his children:

> A scan showed that a major part of the blood supply to the third leg was provided by the girl. . . . The chances were slightly better that the leg would survive . . . on the girl. Your grandfather and your mother had a private meeting with Dr. Thakkar. I wasn't asked to come. . . . I couldn't believe what she told me—that they would risk giving both legs to the boy. . . . The doctor had agreed. . . . It was later I came to know of his intention of starting a large nursing home—the largest in Bangalore. He had acquired three acres of prime land—in the heart of the city—from the state. Your grandfather's political influence had been used. . . . Chandan had two legs for two days. It didn't take them very long to realize what a grave mistake they had made. The leg was amputated. A piece of dead flesh which could have—might have—been Tara. (378)

This long and moving speech by Mr. Patel sums up the entire essence of the play. The play centres around the theme that how the physical separation manipulated by their mother and grandfather to favour the boy (Chandan) over the girl (Tara) results in an emotional separation between the two conjoined twins.

Tara, a feisty girl who isn't given enough opportunities given to her brother, eventually wastes away and dies. Chandan escapes to London, changes his name to Dan and attempts to repress the guilt he feels over his sister's death. His sense of trauma and anguish is so intense that at the end of the play, we see Chandan apologizing to Tara in the most moving of all the lines: "Forgive me, Tara. Forgive me, for making it my tragedy." (380)

Bravely Fought the Queen

Mahesh Dattani is one playwright who is not afraid to work within a relatively conventional society and to tell a story that is bold and powerful. He is one playwright who does not hesitate in mirroring the issue of sexuality, both heterosexuality as well as homosexuality, and presenting it to the audience. Mahesh Dattani in one of his interviews says: "You can talk about feminism, because in a way that is accepted. But you can't talk about gay issues because that's not Indian, [that] doesn't happen here."[18]

Mahesh Dattani boldly portrays homosexuality in his plays and many of his plays like *On a Muggy Night in Mumbai*, *Do the Needful* and *Bravely Fought the Queen* deal with the issue of gays. Mahesh Dattani here can be compared to Oscar Wilde who also presented the stark reality of homosexuality to the Victorians in his novel *The Picture of Dorian Gray*. Wilde had a fascination for young and beautiful men and this homoerotic attitude of Oscar Wilde led to his imprisonment. The novel reveals homoerotic bonds between two men, the well-known artist Basil Hallward and Dorian Gray. Dorian, a beautiful young man, captures Basil's artistic imagination. Dorian sits for several portraits, and Basil often depicts him as an ancient Greek hero or a mythological figure. But the discovery of beauty fading away with time upsets Dorian so intensely that he murders Basil as his paintings would remind Dorian of his once beautiful face when he grows old. The relationship between Basil and Dorian was one of homoeroticism. Dattani's motive in writing such plays is to force society to think about issues that it may not want to deal with.

Mahesh Dattani's lively and provocative play, *Bravely Fought the Queen* charters through the emotional, financial and sexual intricacies of a modern-day Indian family. A cry for the acceptance of shifting Indian values, this play portrays the clash between traditional and contemporary cultures that has created a new social landscape.

Bravely Fought the Queen was written by Dattani in the year 1991 and it was performed at the Sophia Bhabha Hall, Mumbai on 2 August 1991. The play was subsequently performed in 1996 at the Battersea Arts Centre, London, under the aegis of Michael Walling's Border Crossings, UK. Michael Walling while commenting on the British production of *Bravely Fought the Queen* says: "Postcolonial India and multi-cultural Britain both have an urgent need for a cultural expression of the contemporary; they require public spaces in which the mingling of eastern and western influences can take place."[2]

The narrative is centred around an Indian family, in which two brothers, Jiten and Nitin, the co-owners of an advertising agency, have married two sisters, Dolly and Alka. The women remain at lome much of the time, where they look after the men's ageing mother Baa. Baa, white haired in a white sari, wandered constantly through this space, her presence undercutting the apparent naturalism and upsetting the fragile frictions which the characters had created. As Mahesh Dattani says in one of his interviews: "If you look at my plays you would find that each character, every character has, you know, his or her place in the play, which an actor can develop."[20]

So, even if the play like *Tara* is about the twins, the parents have significant parts and also the doctor who did the surgery. In the same way Baa and Praful in *Bravely Fought the Queen* propel events as much as the characters on stage. This kind of genius could be achieved only by a writer like Mahesh Dattani as

Michael Walling points out: "To Mahesh, a play is never really finished. Plays only really happen in the theatre, as ephemeral events. Painstakingly he worked with actors to recreate his text in a form which suited their approach to performance." (229)

It was this kind of skill that made the production of *Bravely Fought the Queen* a success not only in India but in England too. The whole play is beautifully presented in multi-layered levels which again is Dattani's adroitness. The way he juxtaposes the past and the present, the imaginary level and the realistic level without breaking the flow of interest is simply marvellous.

Act 1, "Women," is largely a comedy of manners played between the glacial elder sister Dolly, mischievous dipsomaniac Alka and their unexpected visitor the skittish, ill-at-ease Lalitha. Its final rhapsodic movement paves the way for the second act, in which Jiten, Dolly's husband, is revealed as comprehensively unsympathetic—a violent lecher whose approach to business is a combination of brainless obstinacy and clumsy scams. Jiten's character is somewhat similar to Osborne's character Jimmy in *Look Back in Anger*. Jimmy has been portrayed as a savage and brutal man who inflicts pain on his wife Alison. Both Jimmy and Jiten have been portrayed as unfaithful husbands because Jimmy has an affair with Helena and Jiten gets prostitutes to fulfil his sexual libido. Both the characters have been portrayed as sadists who do not hesitate in hurting the other characters present around them. Jiten epitomizes male chauvinism and reveals it when he says: "Men would want their women dressed up like that. And they have the buying power. Yes! So there's no point asking a group of screwed up women what they think of it." (276)

Jiten represents the conventional male who treats women as sex objects and also gets whores to his office. Baa while describing Jiten says: "Jitu is just like his father. Just like him." (284)

Jiten and Nitin's father was a cruel and a dark man who harassed their mother. The kind of cruelty perpetrated on Baa by her husband is brought to light every now and then in the play when she feels jittery even after so many years of his death: "I have married such a villager! Aah! You slapped me? Never, never slap me. Nobody has hit me. The men in our family are decent." (288)

Baa sees the picture of her husband in her elder son, Jiten and thus automatically develops an inclination towards her younger son, Nitin who resembles her a lot. Nitin is a more subdued and sympathetic character. The mother-son intimacy comes out in the following lines:

> Baa: Nitin! You don't like your father, no? he's not nice! . . . Tell me you hate him! He hits me! Nitin tell me you hate him! Say it!
>
> Nitin: Yes! I hate him! (302)

Baa's story is somewhat similar to that of her daughters-in-law, Dolly and Alka. So here we have two generations sharing the same experiences at the hand of their chauvinistic husbands and a yet to come third generation, Daksha who also experiences the maltreatment of her father even before her birth and is born as a disabled child. Dolly exposes Jiten's cruelty when she says: "And you hit me! Jitu, you beat me up! I was carrying Daksha and you beat me up!" (311)

The result of all this was the premature delivery of Daksha, the disabled daughter of Dolly and Jiten. Then we have Alka, an alcoholic, a boozer who did not prove to be an ideal wife of Nitin but then she raises her voice to question her husband: "I know I haven't been an ideal housewife. . . . And you haven't been . . . well, a competent husband. But who's complaining. Nobody's perfect?" (300)

Women in Mahesh Dattani's plays are not victims. They are marginalized but they fight back. Just like Shashi Deshpande's novel *That Long Silence* tells the story of an Indian housewife who maintained her silence throughout her life in the face of hardships that threatened to break it. *Bravely Fought the Queen* and *That Long Silence* depict the plight of educated Indian women of our time.

Tara, in the play *Tara*, doesn't see herself as a victim, she fights back till the end, she spits her anger every now and then on the outside world. She stays very aloof and the only people she loves interacting with are her parents and her brother. She stands strong and does not get perturbed when people make fun of her physical disability.

In the same way Dolly and Alka in *Bravely Fought the Queen* arm themselves at the end of the play to fight back. Alka very boldly questions the authority of her husband and asks for an explanation for his disloyalty. She also exposes the betrayal of her brother for not revealing the existence of homosexual relations between her husband and her brother.

All the women characters in *Bravely Fought the Queen* are examples of exploitation prevalent in educated urban families and also the examples that women will fight back if they are not heard or are suppressed for a very long time. As Simone de Beauvoir perceives and comments: "The position that women occupy in the society is comparable in many respects to that of racial minorities in spite of the fact that women constitute numerically at least half of the human race."[21]

Mahesh Dattani portrays his women and their fantasies very candidly as he tells Lakshmi Subramanyam in an interview: "I believe I can forget my own gender . . . so those scenes between women didn't come from an 'outside' viewpoint at all." (130)

Baa and Dolly's exploitation is somewhat similar but it is Alka whose anguish and frustration is due to her husband's homosexual libido and her brother Praful's deceit of not revealing the reality of Nitin to her. She takes out her resentment in the end when she says: "The saint gives sister to the sinner and disappears! Finished. Matter over. . . . The saint has another sister who is bad, bad, bad. He beats her till she gets better. And he has this friend. A best friend! The sinner's brother turns out to be his best friend. Not such a coincidence." (300)

Then there was Kanhaiya, who represents the world of sexuality whether heterosexuality or homosexuality. He might be the alluring cook who might or might not be Krishna of Dolly and Alka; or the dark auto driver who embodies Nitin's sexual guilt. Nitin at the end of the play exposes his homosexual relations to Alka who is fast asleep after getting drunk: "How can you still love your brother after what he did to you . . .? Don't answer. Just sleep. You always were a heavy sleeper. At times when I used to spend the night at your place . . . I would go back to Praful's room . . . and kneel. . . . Close enough for my breath to fall gently on his face. And he would open his eyes. . . . I loved him too. He is . . . was attractive. . . . He told me to get married. . . . He told me that you knew. That he had told you . . . about me." (314)

Thus we see that women have not been presented as sinners but they suffer because of the men who are part of their lives. As Mahesh Dattani says in an interview to Lakshmi Subramanyam: "I am not sure I have portrayed the women as victims in *Bravely Fought the Queen*. I see men as victims of their own rage and repression. This has serious consequences on the lives of women." (130)

Mahesh Dattani has always been very particular about the correct portrayal of his women characters and he has no biases against them. He says to Lakshmi Subramanyam: "They are humans. They want something. They face obstacles. They will do anything in their power to get it. All I focus on is the powerlessness of these people. . . . And I am not going to change my sensibilities for political correctness either. My only defence is to say that I am not biased against women." (131)

This attitude of Dattani is clearly revealed in the liberating dance of Alka in the rain. This dance of Alka signifies the sense of freedom from the shackles of society. She seems to be getting ready to fight back, with an imaginary sword swinging in her hand, for all that she has suffered.

Just like Girish Karnad's play *Hayavadana*, Dattani's play *Bravely Fought the Queen* questions the patriarchal moral code which demands the faithfulness of a woman to her husband but not the faithfulness of a man to his wife. Alka is all armed to fight back and to question the norms set by men for women and this instantly reminds the readers of Dolly's lines where she says: "And we can all go—bravely fought! Bravely Fought the Queen! Full of many Valour." (296)

Themes

Mahesh Dattani is a contemporary writer who writes specifically in English. His characters are rooted in the urban cosmopolitan setting of modern middle class India. His plays *Tara* and *Bravely Fought the Queen* are set up in the metropolitan city of Bangalore and *On a Muggy Night in Mumbai* is set up in the city of Mumbai. Writing from the late 1980s, Dattani's plays, like Tendulkar's, question some of the norms and conventions of society. In the process interesting questions regarding gender and other issues like homosexuality, lesbianism, child sexual abuse, etc. are thrown up.

Dattani's genius comes from the fact that he is versatile as an artist. He is an actor, director, and playwright, adept at dancing and has even done screenplay for many of the plays. This is the reason that he is India's first playwright writing in English to be awarded the Sahitya Akademi Award.

Dattani, like Shakespeare, writes for the theatre. Shakespeare wrote plays to be performed on stage, in the same way Dattani believes that the written texts are fully realized only through the process of performance. And so he manages the stage performances of his plays meticulously. Here Dattani is similar to Bernard Shaw who also gives full description of rooms, persons and vital actions. Dattani, like Shaw, uses the stage to condemn many of the drawbacks prevailing in the society. Ibsen, Shaw and Dattani are similar in the sense that all three of them have dealt with women's issues strongly and all three of them have tried to work for the cause of women.

The best aspect of Dattani's plays is that they represent the contemporary society, mainly the urban society. Here Dattani can be compared to Bernard Shaw who also represented his society in his plays and exposed the evils prevalent at the time in his plays like *The Devil's Disciple*, *The Doctor's Dilemma*, *Candida*, *Pygmalion*, and *Mrs. Warren's Profession*. He deals with issues which are very much a part of the educated urban society but the people do not want to confront them and Dattani provides a platform for these issues, so that the people are aware of the fact that they are a reality and not just the fantasies of a playwright.

Dattani's plays can be said to have been inspired by Ibsen, the Father of Realism. Ibsen dealt with a number of social problems in his plays like *The Pillars of Society*, which deals with women rights, *The Doll's House*, which deals with an incompatible marriage and *The Enemy of the People* deals with political and municipal corruption.

In the same way Dattani handles every problem from gender issues to sexuality. In his play *Tara*, he deals with the issue of gender discrimination, in *Thirty Days of September* he deals with the impact of child sexual abuse, in *Bravely Fought the Queen* and *On a Muggy Night in Mumbai* he very boldly deals with the issue of homosexuality and in his award-winning play *Final Solutions*, he deals with the issue of communalism.

Dattani's achievement as a playwright depends on the fact that his plays are a slice of life. They present reality as it exists. He writes about what he observes and an excellent example of his observation is the play *Thirty Days of September*. Dattani wrote this play after being approached by the NGO-Rahi (Recovery and Healing of Incest). In this play he wished to show the impact of child sexual abuse for which he met seven or eight adult women who spoke to him about their childhood experiences where they were sexually abused by their own family members.

Theatre and of course cinema are two best modes of presenting the reality to the people. Watching something live definitely has a greater impact on the minds of the people than reading. Movies like 'A Monsoon Wedding,' and 'A Thousand Acres' and 'Split Wide Open' are a few of the wonderful movies projecting the kind of evils prevalent in the society. In 'A Monsoon Wedding' the uncle sexually assaults his minor niece, the impact of which can be seen in her adulthood too. 'A Thousand Acres' depicts how the daughters are sexually assaulted by their own father. 'Split Wide Open,' splits wide open many evils which exist in a metropolitan city like Mumbai. It exposes many of the issues like a young beggar girl is sexually assaulted by an old man who takes her home under the pretext of looking after her. Another issue that is brought out is how a young daughter-in-law is forced to have sex with her old father-in-law as the son turns out to be impotent.

The two plays that I have dealt in this project are *Tara* and *Bravely Fought the Queen*. These two plays deal with two most favourite topics of Mahesh Dattani and that is gender issue and homosexuality.

In *Tara*, he presents before the audience the problem that even in an urban family living in a metropolitan city like Bangalore, the parents have their bias towards the son and the daughter is neglected even though she might be smarter than her brother.

Mahesh Dattani is one writer who boldly and unhesitatingly handles the issue of homosexuality in his plays. His play *Bravely Fought the Queen* is about women suffering due to the husband's misdoing and the involvement of one of the husbands into homosexual relationships. *Bravely Fought the Queen* is one play which portrays women exploitation by men since time immemorial. Writers like Kamala Das and Shashi Deshpande have also portrayed the plight of women in their novels *My Story* and *That Long Silence*. Marriage as an institution nauseates Kamala Das because it legitimizes violence and gives men a legal control on women's bodies. Mary Wollstonecraft in her book *A Vindication of the Rights of Woman* addresses marriage as "legalized prostitution" as the husband can do whatever to a woman's body at his own free will. In *Bravely Fought the Queen* we have three generations portraying the exploitation by men and they are Baa, Dolly, Alka and Daksha. The play also reveals the fact that the suppression cannot last long as women will fight back to question the autocracy of men just like in the movies 'Daman,' which exposes the issue of marital rape of a wife by her own husband and 'Astitva' which exposes the fact that physical needs are the prerogatives of only men and they can fulfil it whenever and with whosoever they want to but if a woman expresses her sexual desires she is ostracized and labelled as impious. But in both the movies women fight back after prolonged suppression and find their own way instead of submitting to the choices of their husband or the society at large.

Bravely Fought the Queen also presents the concept of gay culture prevalent in big cities. In this way Dattani presents to us the grey realities of the urban families and the conflicts and dilemmas they face.

There's no topic which has not been handled by Dattani in his plays. One has to just think of it and Dattani has a play on it. Dattani is not only a playwright but also a theatre practitioner like Badal Sircar and his written text comes out best when performed in the theatre. His meticulous direction adds wonders to his written text as Mahesh Dattani believes that his work is complete only when it has been performed in front of the audience.

In order to convey his message to the audience and the reader as well and to make them realize and accept that such things do happen in the society he does not restrict himself to using common Indian day-to-day abuses. While writing plays he explores both the masculine and the feminine self within him. This is why Dattani is held as "a playwright of world stature."

NOTES

1. Adya Rangacharya, *The Natyashastra*, Eng. Trans. with Critical Notes (New Delhi: Munshiram Manoharlal, 1996), p. 1.
2. Bharat Gupt, *Dramatic Concepts: Greek and Indian, A Study of Poetics and Natyashastra* (New Delhi. D.K. Printworld, 1994), p. 86.
3. Mahesh Elkunchwar, *Experimentation in Marathi Theatre* (New Delhi. Maharashtra Information Centre, 1995), p. 22.
4. Harish Trivedi, *Colonial Transactions* (Manchester: Manchester University Press. 1996), pp. 176, 184, 207.
5. Mahesh Elkunchwar, p. 22.
6. Rustom Bharucha, *Rehearsals of Revolution: The Political Theatre of Bengal* (Honolulu: University of Hawaii Press, 1993), p. 127.
7. K.R. Srinivasa Iyengar, *Indian Writing in English* (New Delhi: Sterling, 2001), pp. 730, 731.
8. Published in the *International Herald Tribune*.

9. Lakshmi Subramanyam, ed., *Muffled Voices: Women in Modern Indian Theatre* (New Delhi: Shakti, 2002), p. 134.
10. Mahesh Dattani, *Collected Plays* (New Delhi: Penguin India, 2000), Cover Page.
11. *Ibid.*, Cover Page.
12. Told to Anita Nair during an interview.
13. William Shakespeare, *As You Like It*, Act 2, Scene 7.
14. Marjorie Boulton, *The Anatomy of Drama* (New Delhi: Kalyani, 1996), p. 167.
15. Mahesh Dattani, interview to Indiaexpress.com.
16. Sudhir Kakar, *The Inner World: A Psychoanalytic Study of Childhood and Society in India* (New Delhi. Oxford University Press, 1991), p. 52.
17. Mahesh Dattani, *Collected Plays: Tara* (New Delhi. Penguin India, 2000), pp. 323, 324.
18. Interview, "Mahesh Dattani: Invisible Issues," *Performing Arts Journal.*
19. Mahesh Dattani, *Collected Plays, Bravely Fought the Queen: A Note on the Play* (New Delhi. Penguin India, 2000), p. 229.
20. Interview by Anjum Katyal on 9 August 1999.
21. Jasbir Jain, ed., *Women's Writing: Text and Context* (Jaipur and New Delhi: Rawat, 1996), p. 223.

Identity Crisis of Women in *Tara*

SANGEETA DAS
D.G. College, Kanpur

Tara is an ideal character of Dattani which has been widely applauded and variedly interpreted. Dattani himself has tried to depict the feminine side of oneself which always has to come to terms with the society which favours male in a male-dominated world. No matter how much the world proclaims about woman enfranchisement and feminine liberation, subconsciously all women are aware of the fact that they have to go a long way to break shackles. If ever women will be considered equal to men by men, is a big question to answer.

Tara gives us a glimpse into the modern society which claims to be liberal and advanced in its thought and action. It is therefore evident enough to confirm male chauvinism prevalent in the present society. In a society which claims that its mothers are educated today and have 'Devis' like Durga, Kali, Saraswati, Lakshmi etc. whom not only women but men also pay obeisance, differentiate between a male child and female child. All the propagandas of equality between male and female, equal opportunities to women in all the fields are belied. Dattani has attempted an uphill task of pulling out all the taboo subjects from under the rug and putting them on the stage for the public to review. Considering his foresight, it can be said that young playwrights like Dattani, having guts to bring forth such poignant issues and present them threadbare, should be spawned and encouraged.

Dattani's *Tara* gives us a picture of the helplessness of woman in our society. It has received great applause in foreign countries where students have pointed out Tara and Chandan as two aspects of same personality. As Chandan exists, in writing about himself, writes about Tara to rediscover the neglected half of himself. But Dattani's aim in writing the play was to highlight the preference given to a male child over a female child. Whenever the question of choice comes between male and female, it is the male who is chosen.

The play *Tara* also brings forth the bizarre reality of the woman playing second fiddle to man. It opens with Chandan changed into Dan in order to absolve himself from the guilt of killing his sister. Though the poor soul had nothing to do with his sister's untimely death but he bears the brunt of his grandfather's and mother's cruelty. He feels someway responsible for his sister's death and decides to atone for it. For that reason, he escapes to London and transforms his name from Chandan to Dan and lives a self-condemned life. The viciousness of the grandfather and his mother not only takes away the life of the girl but also ruins the life of the boy who was very much attached to his sister Tara.

The fateful leg which was the cause of Tara's bad health and consequent death could not be given to the boy as it became useless after few days. The leg would have been complete success with Tara's body. It would not only have saved her life but also made her a complete person which she very much desired to be, more than Chandan. Chandan was more complacent with his handicapped life while Tara craved every moment for a complete and normal life. The awareness that she has a handicap and the humiliation meted out to her by Roopa and her friends when she was forced to show her handicapped leg to them was like a dagger-jibe to her heart.

Dattani is known widely for picking up scintillating social problems of which this is perennial and glaring. The preference for the beneficence of the male child while staking the life of the female child is pathetic and takes to culmination the feeling of rejection felt by women in our society. So much for the educational policies framed out for the literacy of the women folk and the society as whole. After self-reliance attained by many women in almost all the fields, if such differentiation is done as in Mahesh Dattani's *Tara*, all the declarations and proclamations are bound to go to the drain.

Patel and Bharati are educated parents and the step taken by them is lamentable. Bharati's father, a resourceful person, is also considered to be one of the factors in this mishap but I should say that it is the ultimate decision of the parents which is effective in the life of their children. If Bharati had been led astray by her father's high-handed decision, why didn't Patel put his foot down and stand against their decision? Isn't a father strong enough to fight any hurdle, no matter how strong it is, for the benefit of his siblings? I strongly condemn such parents and would refute the privilege of parenthood to such parents. The incompatibility, which comes between Patel and Bharati after this operation and its futility, tolls heavily on their later life which becomes full of bickerings and showdowns.

Having proved wrong in her decision on the fateful 'leg', Bharati tries to shed her burden of guilt by showing maternal love and concern for her daughter and to assert her moral superiority over her husband. She also tries to expiate by the act of donating kidney to her daughter which was ultimately futile. Patel on the other hand has no compunction for being party to the wrong decision, thanks to gender patriarchy. He tries to accommodate his son Chandan and plans out his education and career for him.

At one point when Tara refuses to fill forms for college and Chandan does likewise, Patel wants Tara to comply not for her own sake but for the sake of her brother. Patel seems to have ruled out the pangs of guilt from his heart of complicity in the injustice done towards Tara and conveniently shifted it on the shoulders of Bharati and her father. Bharati at least tries throughout her life to make up for the damage done. Tara being a girl has been taken for granted by Patel and all his expectations and dreams rested on Chandan whereas Chandan has been shown a boy of a different mentality. When he finally comes to know about the injustice done towards Tara by their parents and grandfather, he is filled with self-guilt and takes up the burden solely on his own shoulders so much so that he leaves India and escapes to London under the name of Dan. Even today, the girls, most of the time, have to submit to the desires of their parents to see their brothers comfortably settled. The sons may be less talented and less intelligent than their daughters, but parents prefer spending money on sons for they believe that the sons are such assets which would stay with them while the girls would go away to their in-laws. Therefore money spent on girls would prove an unnecessary drain on their purse.

Ours has been a patriarchal society where men have always enjoyed a privileged position. Dattani has cleverly exploited this aspect which still remains like a pockmark on the face of our society.

Tara was more enthusiastic and full of zest and spark of life. She had high aspirations which she could not accomplish because of her handicapped state while the boy was comfortably ensconced and had come to terms with his handicapped life. Why was then Tara denied the privilege of the good 'leg'? It would have remained workable if attached to Tara's body. Its severance not only made Tara handicapped but also endangered her life and consequently she died an early death. Why? Is it because she was a girl? Is being a girl in this society a curse? But do not upholders of the society realize the fact that without girls, and consequently women, the society will ultimately come to a standstill. As it is, the ratio of women compared to men is much less in our country. Why so much partiality and differentiation done to women in a country which has a rich heritage and where women are otherwise placed on a pedestal. This seems sheer mockery and nothing of substance.

Like men, women need space to breathe freely and flourish. Mahesh Dattani has tried to show this by bringing in Dr. Thakkar as a social element with the play. Doctors are thought to be messengers of God because they save lives on this earth. Sometimes, when ordinary human beings falter, it is the doctors who show them the right path. Female foeticide has become very common of late. People have degraded themselves to such an extent that they kill the foetus of the female child even before it takes shape in the uterus.

The government has taken a commendable step by putting ban on such an atrocious practice. Many doctors deny revealing to the parents the identity of the foetus just to save the murder. In this play, Dr. Thakkar belied his godly profession and led himself to be bribed by Bharati's father into becoming an accomplice in the bizárre act of severing the leg. He should have upheld his profession by denouncing the decision at its inception whereas he in a way took Tara's life by severing the leg. His wise decision could have given Tara a safe, secured and complete life. His cruelty not only thwarts Tara's dreams but fills her life with dejection and depression. Her depression made her wish for death than unnecessarily spend money on herself. She also started hating all males including Chandan and Patel. One person she cared for was her mother. Her father's attitude toward their mother filled her with distaste for her father and on one occasion she told Chandan that their father was denying her access to their mother. When Tara comes to know about the complicity of her father, mother and grandfather in denying her a full and happy life, she is devastated and Chandan is filled with self-guilt. He is ashamed of what his parents and grandfather did to Tara. Both turn to each other for support and are shown clinging to each other at the end of the play.

Though this is a play about the injustices done to women, it is also a play about injustice to men such as Chandan. For no fault of his own, he is forced to lead a life of guilt. He could not forgive himself for the atrocity done towards his sister. He considers himself responsible for his sister's death which resulted into his refuge in London. When his father informed him about his mother's death, he refused to come back to India.

Identity crisis is strident in our society. Tara is sacrificed because she was a girl and had no right to have a better life than her brother. The idea of a complete girl-child and an incomplete male-child is so shocking that sacrifice of the girl-child is acceptable than a handicapped male-child. Then the revelation of the futility of the decision is taken with so much coolness that no compunction is shown towards the injustice done to the female-child.

Ours has always been a male-dominated society. The senior male member of the family had made the rules on which the decision has been taken. Even if there happened to be a female member who was elder to the male member, she was not given so much authority as the male. In case of Dattani's *Tara* too, Bharati's father who was senior-most of the three and a powerful and rich politician, was the person who determined about the operation in which the leg was to be given to Chandan instead of Tara. He went as far as bribing the doctor with sanction of land in Bangalore. Dr. Thakkar fell from his high station and without giving a second thought, along with his team, instead of taking a sound medical decision of leaving the leg with Tara, sold out his conscience for his ambitions and the temptation, to people, who had decided on the basis of gender and not on medical grounds.

Bharati's father further strengthened his indulgence for male grandchild by leaving his property after his demise to Chandan and not a single penny to Tara. He has been a consistent upholder of values pertaining to males. Patel's attitude has also been negative. He remained a mute observer of the whole affair. Isn't it because he too subscribes to the ideology of the patriarchal world? He blames his wife and father-in-law for the damage done but his complicity in the whole operation cannot be denied.

The fact that the male is always given the greater chance is obvious from Patel's planning for Chandan's education and future career. Bharati started fawning over Tara because of her sense of guilt but Patel doesn't seem to have cared much about it. It is more of gender patriarchy which dominates the play to underline which Dattani makes Dan apologise to Tara at the end of the play: "Forgive me Tara. Forgive me for making it my tragedy."

After the injustice done, the deficiency is tried to be patched up by love. What we see is that love is an instrument, not an end or a state of being. Men are practical, strong and less emotional than women. Women, when subdued, resort to emotional weapons of which love is one. Bharati uses her love for Tara as a weapon against Patel as well as an expression of her desire to compensate to Tara. Female-children are more sensitive than male-children. Tara is also taken up by her mother's concern and indulgence of her; little did she know that her loving mother was an accomplice in destroying her dreams. Bharati's unnecessary bullying of Roopa into friendship with Tara and trying to bribe her into spending more time with Tara is disgusting and demeaning. Such acts, instead of easing the life of a handicapped child, further push them into the depths of darkness and decline. Can parental love be taken for granted? Can any love be taken for granted as a natural given? Such relationship puts in jeopardy the chances for individual growth and fulfillment.

The revelation of the skeleton in the cupboard is the typical method of a Dattani play. Here the skeleton points towards the gender issue. The whole set-up leads inexorably towards the revelation, and the characters are seen struggling to meet the imminent moment of crisis. Dattani's novels have the quality of unearthing the secrets of the family life of the present day. Each individual is a social element and cannot escape the societal dictates and familial choices.

Tara is neither Chandan's tragedy nor is it really Tara's. The tragic events depicted in the play are the tragic actions belonging to everyday life. It is Dattani's world where the playwright picks up various characters from the society as puppets, makes society the background and displays to us the fiery issues of today. In this play, Dattani became a juggler and juggles with husband and wife relationship, doctor and patient relationship, son-in-law and father-in-law relationship, parents and children relationship, brother and sister relationship, with special focus on father-daughter, mother-daughter and grandfather-granddaughter relationships.

The gender crisis which has given rise to identity crisis among our women folk is heart-rending when so much social propaganda along with prospective marathon undertaking to strengthen women's progress has been proposed in the country's agenda. Dattani has just made the effort to highlight one of the atrocities done towards a female and belie all the hue and cry for female emancipation and equality with men on all grounds.

In *Tara*, physical deficiency has been given too much weight. Tara has been shown helpless because she has a handicap and is consequently denied the privileges of life. But Tara could have made her deficiency, her strength and fight the society to etch a place of her own. She was a bubbly and energetic girl who had all the qualities of a normal girl. If she had been given moral support by her parents, especially her father, she might have shone like a star as her name justifies. Her father's eager planning for her brother's future and total ignorance towards her forced her to believe that she was incompetent for any productive work. In short, her life was a burden on this earth. This made her lose interest in life altogether. Further she refuses to go to physiotherapy or fill forms for college.

Through Dattani's *Tara*, we come to know about the sincerity and inclination of a girl to prove her mettle in the world of male supremacy. As the name Tara rightfully suggests a star, the girl was a bright and shinning star which was a source of cheerfulness and happiness of the family. A complete life could have done wonders and surely she would have scored the limits which her brother Chandan couldn't have. Chandan did not have the fire in him which Tara had. The character Roopa has been included in the play by Dattani to show the futility of fullness in that girl. She, though normal, was offensive and comic. Her presence makes the reader feel the waste of fullness in her and bitterness of Tara's deficiency. Tara has been depicted as a female character with potential while her brother was not enterprising at all but the father of the two was bent upon securing the future of the boy. Tara's potentiality was sacrificed on the altar of gender. Identity crisis becomes a chain with which a female is fettered when the question of choice between male and a female arises.

Dattani has been successful in hitting the target by writing the play *Tara*. He has not only focused on the futility of capacities in the girl but has also tried to show the pathetic humiliation faced by a handicap through the incident when Tara had to expose her artificial leg to the three girls in her locality. Tara is hurt and in her moment of deep hurt and resentment caused by the 'normal' world she wants to hear only Beethoven. She identifies herself with the musician with a disability who established his greatness in spite of being unable to hear his own creations.

Thus, Dattani's target—gender-identity leading to identity crisis in women—has been deftly revealed in this play. Certain questions spring up in our minds such as: How are men and women constructed in terms of gender? What are the definitions of their roles? How meaningful are these definitions? What is manly and what feminine? Why it should be so? Why can't women go out in the world? Why should men be masterly and women subservient? Why can't men and women be open about their sexuality? Dattani raises these and host of other questions regarding gender and social stratification and hierarchy and sexuality but has left them to be answered by us. We have to ponder over these issues.

The (Un)twinkling Star: Who Takes Tara's Shine Away?

SUBHASH CHANDRA
S.B.S. College, University of Delhi

Mahesh Dattani, who is known for bringing into the open those questions/issues which the Indian society and culture tends to brush into the garbage pail, because they are uncomfortable, has written and produced the play *Tara,* which has several entry points.

The play can be approached through the issue of simple man-woman relationship (of course unequal in our patriarchal system, like other countries), or it can be responded to in terms of the disabled children's struggle against a variety of odds, which have been put in their way by nature, or chance, or accident of their birth. Or one can respond to the text through the positioning of the girl-child in Indian culture and society.

The man-woman relationship is dramatized through the interactions between Mr. Patel and his wife Bharati. He is shown to be often rude and authoritarian, when it comes to dealing with her and taking decisions. Of course, he turns out to be a caring husband, too, in his looking after Bharati during her bouts of depression. His words about Bharati reveal his concern: "Maybe I'm expecting the worst. It may never happen—no. Things are getting out of hand. I must worry about her. Yes. I am worried—about my wife."[1] But at the same time, he exhibits a streak of harshness, even heartlessness towards her. His admonition to Bharati not to give one of her kidneys to Tara who needs a kidney transplant, is not the result of his concern for his wife's health, but is the product of his cruel attitude towards her. When questioned by Bharati why he is against it, his answer is in keeping with his overall treatment of his wife: "Because I do not want you to have the satisfaction of doing it." (344) This quite negates his professed concern which he talks about when Bharati is in the throes of depression. Similarly, he deprives Bharati of the chance to confess her sin to Tara which she has committed towards her (Tara). That would have relieved her guilt and possibly her malady, but it seems that he does not want relief for her. His words sound heartless: "No. I don't want to give her the satisfaction of confessing." (377) His summary dismissal of Bharati's opinions as inconsequential and not paying heed to her expostulations on behalf of Tara represent him as a typical overriding patriarchal husband. It is another matter that we come to know later why Bharati was rabidly trying to champion Tara's case—it is not for the sake of Tara that she does it. It is more for herself, as would become clear later in the essay. However, with Bharati's underlying motive for her effusions of love towards Tara becoming clear, the play does not linger on intensively on the unequal relationship between the husband and wife. This, therefore, is not the central strand, determining the progress of the plot.

The theme of odds faced by the physically challenged children (or adults) in society no doubt comes through. Tara's artificial leg, the ridicule she is subjected to by her peers at school and in the neighbourhood (by Roopa, Prema and Nalini—the last two do not appear on the stage) and the limp caused by the artificial leg which symbolically serves as the marker of a disadvantage compared to others are indicative of the playwright's interest in this issue. Roopa's words about Tara are representative of the attitude of Prema and Nalini, and possibly of the society at large: "She is a real freak of nature all right." (342) But in this case, too, we find that this disability does not pose an insurmountable challenge to Tara, who has the capacity to laugh at it herself, and laugh at the imbecility of those who consider it great deprivation and a subject of pity or ridicule. She is very much capable of holding her own and making the best of her life, with all its givens. This, too, therefore, does not frame the whole of the play, demanding detailed attention.

I would, therefore, like to use the last prism, that is, the positioning of the girl-child in Indian society to enter the text and raise the following questions: Who has killed Tara? And why?

Before I take up the discussion in detail, I would like to mention an anecdote (based on personal experience) because it is quite relevant to the position I take in the essay. Our washerwoman used to bring a small sickly girl child along, when she came to collect clothes. The child was her granddaughter (her son's daughter). Rheumy in the eyes, and wearing shabby frocks, the child seemed to be ill. When my wife asked her the reason for her sad condition, the old woman casually replied that the child was like that from birth. And then she came without the child one day. On enquiry, we learnt that she had died. No grief or remorse on the old woman's face. She talked as chirpily as ever. After a couple of years, she carried a boy-infant in the crook of her arm. But that is another story. Here what is relevant is who killed the small girl child? And why?

The answer to this question and the one emerging from the textual exploration of the play, *Tara,* would be the same.

I would like to argue in the course of the essay that it is not one individual who has killed Tara. It is the socio-cultural system which is responsible for her death. The beliefs, the attitudes, and the prejudices that are deep-rooted in the collective Indian cultural psyche become instrumental in taking Tara's life. It is a complex play. Issues of class and community interplay to weave the plot of the play and bring about the climactic moment of reversal of expectations. This reversal of expectations in the matter of Bharati, Tara's mother, who sympathized with Tara actually is not the central point the play makes. .

Coming to the question who has killed Tara, it is proper to know who Tara is, what her background is, in what sort of family, neighbourhood and society she is born and lives and dies. She is a Siamese twin, born to the Patels—Mr. Patel (his first name is not given) and Bharati, his wife. Born conjoined as one body with her brother Chandan, she is separated by a complicated, technologically advanced surgical operation by Dr. Thakkar who is visiting India from London. The discrimination against her begins right from the process of surgery. I would revert to it later, but I would like to mention in passing the three levels on which Tara is deprived of what is her due: (i) at the hands of Nature, which makes her weaker and reduces the chances of her survival. In Dr. Thakkar's words: "Our greatest challenge would be to keep the girl alive. Nature wanted to kill her. We couldn't allow it." (376) (ii) At the level of society whose attitude is reflected through her peers—her classmate in class nine, Roopa and her friends Prema and Nalini, who find amusement in her wooden leg. (iii) At the level of family, especially at the hands of her mother and maternal grandfather—they deprive her of one of the two healthy legs. Briefly going over the three levels of discrimination, we find that it is the last which would need detailed consideration:

1. Discrimination against her by nature is accidental. Generally, born as single children, girls have better chances of survival than boys. But in this case, Tara happens to be the weaker of the two twins.
2. As far as discrimination by the society is concerned, as mentioned earlier, Tara is not overly disturbed what others think of her infirmity. Therefore, it is almost insignificant.
3. Discrimination by the family is a serious matter, as it is conscious and is the result of a conspiracy against her. At the time of surgical separation from her brother, a conspiracy is hatched against her by none else than her very own mother, Bharati, who has conceived and produced her, her grandfather (maternal) and Dr. Thakkar. She gets deprived of one of the two healthy legs. The Siamese twins had three healthy legs. One of the healthy legs had greater chances of survival on the girl child as the blood supply to it came from the girl's body. But Tara was not given her due. She was deprived of what was hers because Bharati wanted to have a healthy and able son. So, Chandan was given the two healthy legs. This conspiracy needs to be commented upon in the light of what happens to the girl child in Indian society.

There is no specific and clear answer because there cannot be one. No one individual is responsible for what happens to her, because this has to do with the positioning of the girl-child in the Indian society.

The point I am trying to make is that all types of discrimination Tara faces at the hands of her family members (and the family needs to be considered as a microcosm of society) are the consequence of their being prisoners in the hands of collective unconscious that constitutes their psyches. The sources of this collective unconscious are the cultural/religious texts which determine Indians' attitudes towards women. It would be appropriate to recall what Manu, the powerful Indian sage, has to say about women. In his words:

> In childhood must a female be dependent on her father, in youth, on her husband; her lord being dead, on her sons, if she has no sons, on the near kinsmen of her husband; if she be left no kinsmen, on those of her father; if she has no paternal kinsmen, on the sovereign; a woman must never seek independence. (V, 148)

Women were not admitted to the Sangha[3] because the company of women was considered to be an obstacle in the attainment of higher powers in man. This is what Buddha, one of the most egalitarian prophets had to say about women:

> Women are soon angered, Ananda,
> Women are full of passion, Ananda,
> Women are envious, Ananda, women are stupid.
> That is the reason, Ananda, that is the cause,
> Why women have no place in public assemblies, do not carry on
> Business, and do not earn their living by any profession.[4]

Let us examine the positioning of the girl child in Indian society and then see what happens to Tara and that would give us the answer to the crucial question who has killed Tara and why.

What happens to the girl child in the Indian society? She faces infanticide (now she undergoes feticide, thanks to the evolved technology) and if by chance she is born, she is abandoned either to die, or to be picked up by an orphanage or by a needy couple (who want a boy child) and or compassionate couple (their number is woefully small) who just want a child. More often than not, the abandoned girl child dies. Ironically, this happens in a society, which has a mythology, with goddesses being worshipped as Kali and Durga (shakti), Saraswati (as wisdom) and Lakshmi (as wealth). Indian society which seeks to occupy high moral ground through its belief in the concept of '*vasudhev kutumbkam*' does not hesitate in exterminating its daughters by short term or long-term means. The effect of this type of treatment of girl child was visible in the last census. The number of girls in relation to boys per thousand has alarmingly reduced. Strangely enough, the worst culprits in this matter are Punjab and Haryana—the two most prosperous states of India. India's self-righteous, sanctimonious and ennobling social concepts do not lend security to the girl child.

There are two pointers in the play which make me believe that Dattani also wants us to interpret it along the lines of the social system being the culprit in the matter of cruelty to girl children. The following conversation between Chandan and Roopa serve as one pointer:

Chandan: What would you □o if you had to choose between a boy and a girl? Who would you choose?

Roopa. I think it's more civilized to drown her (girl) in milk. (365)

Chandan and Tara's maternal grandfather was a wealthy man. He was in politics and came very close to becoming the Chief Minister. His will is a testament of the kind of treatment that is meted out to girls in Indian society. Mr. Patel and Chandan are talking:

Patel: He [grandfather] left you a lot of money.

Chandan: And Tara?

Patel: Nothing.

Chandan: Why?

Patel: It was his money. He could do what he wanted with it. (360)

The worst part is that this conversation takes place in the presence of Tara. No consideration whatsoever for her feelings! Tara is the victim of this collective social system.

Having been successfully separated from her twin brother, her ordeal continues. We have talked about the conspiracy of her own mother against her. Her father, Mr. Patel, is not much different from his wife, though Bharati is guilty of a more serious crime/sin against Tara. He continuously and doggedly favours Chandan when it comes to giving him higher education abroad, and a career. (Patel: "Chandan is going to study further and he will go abroad for his higher studies." [352]) Tara is discouraged openly, notwithstanding her feelings in the matter, even though she is more intelligent, sharp and witty and would perform well if given opportunities in life. It is only when Chandan refuses to go College without her, Patel thinks of sending Tara, too, to college. Bharati supports Tara in the matter of higher education and in some other cases, but her support is tainted. It is the product of the guilt and cannot be interpreted as fighting the systemic odds in Tara's way. Helena Michie's concept of "domestic carceral" is relevant here, though she has used it in a different context (in the context of women's pregnancy.) She says: "The phrase 'domestic carceral' points to women's imprisonment in the home and in the marriage plot and away from teleology which seems home and marriage as benign alternatives . . . to a world of robbers and rapists who come in from outside."[5]

Economic and religious/cultural factors have been responsible for the antipathy against and inferiorization of the girl child. (It should be noted that this phenomenon of inferiorization of girl/woman is not peculiar to India alone.) A boy helps in contributing to the family income, whether by working in the field, or elsewhere. It is through him that the *vansh* (clan) continues, because of the patriarchal system which requires the members of the family to carry caste names, coming from the father (male side). Parents can attain *moksha* only if a son does the '*kapaal kriya*' (breaking of the skull while being cremated). So, either girls are killed at birth, or abandoned. The medical and technological advances have made it possible to detect the sex of the fetus. This has given an impetus to the killing of the girls, as mentioned above. All these factors combine to create the social system in which the girl child has to live and die.

Tara is killed by the social system, which controls the minds and actions of people. The trauma of coming to know the role her mother had played in her life, and the discrimination she faces at the hands of her father and grandfather become too much for her. And why is she killed? Tara is not wanted. Girls are not wanted. They are irrelevant from the points of view of religion and economics. They are dispensable.

It is noteworthy that discrimination against Tara continues even after her death. Chandan, who was always interested in writing, and who has come to England for higher studies, has transformed into Dan. He turns the story he writes into his own tragedy. It is only incidentally that he has to tell Tara's story, too. Dan apologizes to Tara for doing this: "Forgive me, Tara. Forgive me for making it my tragedy." (380) It is quite another matter that it becomes Tara's tragic story also. But that is only incidental.

The play presents a mirror to the Indian society (to use a cliché) to see its true face. It tries to shock the society out of its grooved thinking. Through racy dialogue and bare minimum stage-setting (by just picking out the characters through cross-fadings of light) the playwright effectively portrays the interactions among the characters. The authenticity of the play is established by making Chandan (Chandu at home and later called Dan after his arrival in England) as the narrator/writer of the play. He is one of the Siamese twins (the other twin being Tara, his sister) and nobody could know better than he does. .

Taras (stars) do not twinkle on the Indian sky! Because they are not allowed to!!

NOTES

1. Mahesh Dattani, *Tara* in *Collected Plays* (New Delhi: Penguin: 2000), p. 330.
2. This is what Joseph Conrad has to say about women: "It is queer how out of touch with truth women are. They live in a world of their own, and there has never been anything like it, and can never be." (*Heart of Darkness*).

3. Later Buddha permitted women to join Sangha for the development of their spiritual powers.
4. Tara Ali Baig, *India's Women Power* (New Delhi: S. Chand, 1976), p. 57.
5. Helena Michie, "The Domestic in the Discourses of Upper-Middle-Class Pregnancy," *Feminisms: An Anthology of Literary Theory and Criticism*, ed. Robyn R. Warhol and Diane Price Herndl (Hampshire: Macmillan, 1997), p. 58.

Mahesh Dattani's *Dance Like a Man*: An Analysis in Technique and Theme

B. YADAVA RAJU
P.G. College, Osmania University

The plays of Mahesh Dattani bring Indian English Drama into the post-Nineties. His plays are so realistic that sometimes they generate a lot of discussion and controversy. At the same time, his plays embody many of the classical concerns of world drama. Human relationships and family unit have always been at the heart of his dramatic representation. While concentrating on the family unit and human relationships, Dattani bravely experiments with the techniques of presentation. He often uses split-scenes, hidden rooms and many other innovations. In *Dance Like a Man*, Dattani makes use of the 'flash-back' technique and the split-scene device. The scene is arranged in a living room of a dimly lit room in an old-fashioned house in the heart of a city. Just behind the entrance of the room, a modern-looking rear panel is arranged. When specified in the script the rear panel is slid to reveal a garden. The garden represents the past and all the events of the past life invariably take place in the garden. As opposed to this, the living room in the house represents the present. All events pertaining to the present take place here. Thus a split-scene is a convenient device to move the action between the present and the past.

Another dramatic device Dattani makes use of in the play is regarding the roles of the actors. The play requires four actors, and the roles that are played by each actor are arranged like this:

1. The Young Man, in his early twenties, plays Viswas and the younger Jairaj.
2. The Young Woman, in her early twenties, plays Lata and the younger Ratna.

3. The Old Man, in his early sixties, plays the older Jairaj and his father, Amritlal Parekh.
4. The Old Woman, in her early sixties, plays the role of older Ratna Parekh.

Mahesh Dattani gives much importance to this role switching and expects that this is adhered to carefully as it is 'vital to the structure' of the play. The present paper attempts to analyze the play in two sections. Section I deals with the present developments of the play, while section II deals with the past events of the play.

I

The play opens with the living room in an old-fashioned house. Viswas and Lata Parekh enter the room. The occasion is going to be a sort of assessment by the Parekhs of their future son-in-law. But, unfortunately, one of their musicians has met with an accident and both Jairaj Paresh and Ratna Parekh have gone to the hospital. Meanwhile, Lata Parekh and Viswas are seen engaged in a conversation that gradually unfolds the details of the Parekhs. Lata's parents, Jairaj Parekh and Ratna Parekh, are dancers like Lata. Lata tells Viswas that her parents are of a 'different'[1] type. The house in which they are living is forty to fifty years old. Being located in the centre of the city, there seems to be a lot of demand for the site of the house. But Jairaj is not willing to sell it because of certain sentimental reasons, according to Lata. Lata further tells Viswas that her parents learnt and danced together under the same guru in that house. As a little girl Lata used to watch her parents practise dancing. It was 'magic' (114) for her to do so. She tells Viswas that her father is a 'bit more pliable than usual' (118) and her grandfather, who was a freedom fighter and social reformer who became busy later 'handling' his son who was wanting to be a dancer. In spite of the old man's resistance to (his son's) dancing, according to Lata, Lata's father had deep respect for the old man. While Lata was making coffee in the kitchen, Viswas looks around the room and finds a large ornate cupboard. He opens the cupboard and removes a "splendid brocade shawl." (121) He tells Lata that he is going to ask for the 'shawl' as dowry. But Lata warns Viswas by informing him that her father will not like to part with the shawl because he is very fond of it, and it is his "most prized possession." (121) After some time, Viswas once again takes out the 'shawl,' wears it and struts around without being noticed by Lata. He goes on imitating the old man in a mock fatherly voice. It is exactly at this moment Jairaj Parekh and Ratna Parekh enter and stare at Viswas's antics. Viswas is embarrassed to find them staring at him and offers some explanation. But Jairaj and Ratna are not in a position to pay attention to what Viswas is saying. They seriously discuss the problem of Lata's dance performance. The indisposition of Mr. C.V. Srinivas, their mridangist, has thrown up a crisis as to who would be a suitable substitute in his absence. Especially Ratna Parekh is so worried that the attempts of Jairaj Parekh to calm her down backfire on him, and Ratna begins to blame Jairaj and his father, Amritlal Parekh, for their present lot. She accuses Jairaj for being a 'spineless boy' who could not leave his father's house for more that forty-eight hours. (132) Jairaj complains that Ratna has been holding this against him for the last forty years. It is in this way that the past is brought to bear its mark on the present. The audiences gradually come to understand that the relationship between Jairaj and Ratna is not a smooth and healthy one. Fretting and fuming Ratna exits to her bedroom. Having watched all this, Viswas tries to leave the house. But Jairaj stops him and offers him drinks and also tells him about his father, Amritlal Parekh, "the setji of the city." (136) What the audiences understand from this is that there is a lot of dislike and disregard between the father and the son. This view is quite different from what Lata has explained to Viswas so far. Jairaj Parekh further tells Viswas that he was trying to 'remove all the memories' of his father, including his "gardening." (138) Then Viswas asks about 'the shawl' and the reason for keeping it. Jairaj doesn't answer this question, but agrees to give it to Viswas after his marriage with Lata.

Ratna re-enters with the same proposal that was suggested by Jairaj that they could ask Chandra Kala to lend Mr. Seshadri. With this proposal, the solution to the present crisis has been found. But once again they dig up their past life. Now, it is Jairaj, who begins, and asks Ratna how they could have continued to live with her uncle especially after he had asked his niece Ratna to go to bed with him? (143) He tries to clarify to Ratna that her uncle's behaviour was the reason behind Jairaj's returning to his father's house. Both of them agree that to leave Amritlal Parekh's house was an 'impulsive' (144) decision. But with the mention of 'Shankar,' the chasm between them is once again revealed. Just before retiring to his bedroom, Jairaj notices the 'shawl.' He picks it up and tries to put it into the cupboard, but changes his mind and speaks to himself:

> Your last memory. Soon I'll be rid of you too. Then I won't see you wearing this shawl, walking about this room. . . . Walking about—wearing this shawl. (146)

Thus the entire present part of Act One shows the not-so-healthy kind of relationship between Jairaj and Ratna. At this stage, the audiences have no clue to either the name of 'Shankar,' or to the mystery of the 'shawl.'

The present part comes to an end with the living room portion changing into a lovely rose-garden. The spotlight picks up a young man with 'jathis' being recited in background. The characters also change. Jairaj becomes the father Amritlal Parekh, Viswas becomes young Jairaj, Lata young Ratna. The time of the action is nineteen forties. The second section of this paper deals with this part, that is, 'the past' of the play.

The present part of Act Two opens with a telephone ringing in the living room. Ratna picks up the phone. She is seen receiving the calls from all the VIPs of the city. She is congratulated on the success of her daughter, Lata Parekh's dance performance. All the newspapers like *Herald*, *The Times* and *The Express* have published favourable, rave reviews about the dance performance. Jairaj and Viswas are very excited about the reviews. Lata Parekh is described as 'the star of the Festival,' 'A Shining Star in the sky of Bharatnatyam,' etc. Lata, Viswas and Jairaj are reading the reviews. Lata says that these rave reviews are her mother's 'efforts' (174). But Jairaj would not 'give her the credit entirely' (174).

Viswas's ignorance about dance is exposed in the ensuing conversation. One of the reviewers comments on Lata's rendition of 'the ashtapadi' from *Geet Govindam.* The reviewer praises Lata's 'tearful expression,' (175) and says that her 'heaving bosom conveyed all that was humanly possible.' (175) But Lata clarifies that her bosom was heaving because 'She was breathless' from the 'varnam.' But Viswas does not like this comment saying that 'it was too erotic.' (176) Lata understands that Viswas, like many people, has his own 'quirks' (178) about dance. Thus, Dattani makes it clear that the misconceptions about Bharatnatyam continue till today. Later, a verbal duel takes place between Jairaj and Ratna, contesting the rave reviews. While Ratna thinks that the reviews are because of her own 'efforts,' Jairaj refutes this opinion and asserts that Lata 'deserved' (183) them. According to Jairaj, the reviewers were not doing Ratna 'any favour.' (183) In this connection he tells Ratna that "at least [she] has a daughter to be jealous of." (184)

With this comment the scene once again moves back to the past when Ratna just returned from a dance programme with a splendid Bharatnatyam costume, and a 'shawl' covering all this. Once again the living room changes into a rose-garden and the characters also change accordingly. Thus, the tension-ridden, distrustful and suspicious life of the artists is exposed in the present part. The audience is left in a suspense regarding the reasons for the suspicious, distrustful and anxiety-ridden life of these characters.

II

The second part of Act One of the play deals with the conflict between art and society, and it also focuses on the sense of competition and anxiety among the artists themselves. Young Jairaj and Ratna are practising dance in the house of Amritlal Parekh, who is a representative of the society of the Nineteen thirties and the forties. He is a freedom fighter and a reformist, but curtails the freedom of his son, who wants to become a male

Bharatnatyam dancer. Amritlal Parekh is an autocratic father for whom Bharatnatyam is the "craft of prostitute to show off her wares," (137) hence a man has no business to learn such a craft, and anyone who "learnt such a craft could not be a man." (137) Amritlal Parekh approves of the marriage between Jairaj and Ratna, according to Jairaj, because it "suited [his] image—that of a liberal minded person, to have a daughter-in-law from outside [his] community." (150) But Amritlal never thought that the interest of his son in dance "would turn into an obsession." (149) According to Jairaj, Amritlal Parekh "was as conservative and prudish" as the white rulers. (150)

In the earlier days Bharatnatyam was associated with temples and rituals. The art was preserved by 'devadasis,' who were professional dancers in temples. They were, however, exploited by the priests and rulers, and eventually, out of economic necessity, turned to prostitution. Hence, a stigma came to be attached to the dance form itself. Till nineteen thirties and forties, the dance form was ignored and neglected. Added to this was the British prudish attitude, which dubbed Bharatnatyam as 'erotic.' Some of our 'brown sahibs' also endorsed such views and considered the art form as a 'debased and licentious remnant' of our barbaric past (see the playwright's 'Note' to the play). The anti-nautch movement of the nineteen thirties further whipped public opinion up against this art form. But in spite of this, in the same decade, a few young dancers from well-to-do and respectable families came forward to learn the art form from the 'devadasis.'

The play focuses on this conflict in the character like Amritlal Parekh who represents the attitudes of the older generation of the society during the Thirties and Forties. The younger generation, represented by Jairaj and Ratna, oppose such an attitude. Jairaj and Ratna challenge the old man who has no good opinion about the art form. Amritlal even suspects Ratna's attempts to learn 'the Mysore school of dance' from Chenniamma, who is a seventy-five years old living exponent of the art form. As a result of this tussle, Jairaj and Ratna leave the house in defiance. The first flashback of Act One ends with this defiance.

Act Two continues with the flashback of Act One focusing on the events of the forties. Jairaj and Ratna, out of sheer helplessness return to Amritlal Parekh's house within two days. Their helplessness is exploited by Amritlal Parekh who imposes certain restrictions on them. He tells Jairaj 'not to grow his hair any longer' (164) and asks Ratna 'not to learn [any dance] from anyone else (164). He further informs Ratna that man's happiness lies 'in being a man.' (164) He assures Ratna that *she* would be allowed to dance if she helps him, in making Jairaj 'an adult' (166) who could be worthy of a woman. After this kind of agreement with Ratna, the old man disappears from the scene. It appears as if he has handed over this responsibility to Ratna. Ratna, thus, buys her freedom to dance at the expense of Jairaj's desire to become a male Bharatnatyam dancer. Ambition overtakes Ratna. In order to prove herself to be a dancer, she 'destroys' Jairaj by undermining his 'self-esteem' (188) as an artist.

In the second flashback of Act Two, the way in which this plan of 'destruction' has been executed is dramatized. Jairaj feels neglected and dismissed. He feels that he is used as a tool, as a stage prop, or as a choreographer to Ratna's dance-items, but seldom as a co-dancer. One day Ratna returns from a dance programme with a splendid Bharatnatyam costume, and a shawl covering all this. Jairaj follows her in a drunken condition. It is obvious that Ratna continues her dance practice and gives several performances, whereas Jairaj becomes only a stage prop. Thus, the 'shawl' stands as a symbol of Jairaj's unfulfilled desire to be recognized as a dancer. Ratna scolds Jairaj for his drunkenness and asks him to do 'something useful before it is too late' (187), and 'stop the mockery.' But Jairaj holds Ratna responsible for his drunkenness because, he says, he is deprived of dancing. Ratna retorts Jairaj blaming him for his addiction to alcohol and for his 'mediocrity.' (190) She also holds Amritlal Parekh responsible for Jairaj's downfall. According to Ratna, Jairaj's downfall begins from the day he returned to his father's house. She charges that he has always been "a spineless boy" who couldn't "leave his father's house for more than forty-eight hours." (132) For her, Jairaj 'stopped being a man' from that fateful day onwards. For the past forty years Ratna has been holding this complaint against Jairaj. In fact, the audience gets to know about this mutual disagreement and distrust between Jairaj and Ratna in their very first meeting with them in Act One. The play opens with this distrust between them and continues to show it till the end of the play.

Jairaj hopes that he would teach his son, little Shankar, the dance "of Shiva, the dance of man." (185) He wishes that Shankar would dance the 'tandava nrityam' (185) right on the head of his grandfather, when he becomes a young man. But this desire of Jairaj also remains unfulfilled because the child dies in his childhood. It appears that the ayah, in an attempt to keep the child away from weeping for his mother, administers an overdose of opium and unknowingly kills the child. According to Jairaj, Ratna is more responsible for the death of the child. He alleges that Ratna was always after the name and fame as a dancer rather than discharging her duty as a mother and as a wife.

Thus there has been a mutual distrust and disagreement between Jairaj and Ratna. This distrust between them is born out of Ratna's ambition. The unison and 'jathi,' that are required in any successful dance item, are lacking in their day-to-day life. They might have succeeded as dancers, but have failed as human beings, a wife and husband. The play ends with Jairaj's admission that they were only human and lacked the 'grace,' 'brilliance' and 'magic' to dance like God. (194) To be able to revise, protect and continue any art form, the artist(s) should rise above the human weaknesses. Art can only be protected in the hands of such artists.

NOTE

1. Mahesh Dattani, *Final Solutions and Other Plays* (Manas Imprint, Delhi: Rupa, 1994), p. 113.

Where There is a Will and *Bravely Fought the Queen*: The Drama of Mahesh Dattani

SUBIR DHAR
Rabindra Bharati University, Calcutta

Mahesh Dattani is the Sachin Tendulkar of English language drama in India. And in case this comparison seems extravagant, it may be pointed out that in Dattani we have a playwright whose accomplishments in the field of theatre have been compared not only with those of such stellar luminaries as Henrik Ibsen and Tennessee Williams, but also a practitioner of stagecraft who has been lauded for his "adventurous . . . ways of using theatrical space."[1] Certainly the talents of this still young dramatist are considerable. For one thing, the stage for him is no undifferentiated flat platform, but far more vitally, a complex multi-dimensional zone in which events held in time may be framed and re-framed, viewed and re-viewed, regarded and re-regarded; an arena of performance in which such neglected (in theatre, at least) realities as humidity and air-temperature are given much importance in performance as the props on a stage[2]; a space in which the writing of the words of a play-text imperceptibly takes on the flesh of an enactment,[3] and the use of masks and dance-like movements take on the significance of deeper ritualistic meanings.[4]

Dattani has been seen too as a radical challenger of "the construction of 'India' and 'Indian,' as they have traditionally been defined in modern theatre."[5] And this observation signposts us into the area of this playwright's topics or subjects of dramatization which are (or more correctly, have been till date) social, cultural, sexual and religious issues. Dattani's earliest performed play, *Where There is a Will* (1988) is a comedy with slight farcical touches which yet makes a point about the way patriarchal men invariably fail to exist as true human beings. The plot of this play revolves around the life (and more importantly, after-life) of a man named Hasmukh Mehta, who is a rich and successful businessman, and his family. The action starts with Hasmukh, having come home from office, overhearing his twenty-three-year-old son and Joint Managing Director of his firm complaining about his father's refusal to invest in new business ventures thought up by him. In a series of straight addresses or asides to the audience, Hasmukh clarifies that he had thrown away his son Ajit's project proposals unread because "If I let him have his way, we would all be paupers." Ajit, he plaintively adds, "was bankrupt up here (*points to his head*) the day he was born. God just forgot to open an account for him."[6]

Neither does Hasmukh have any love to spare for his wife Sonal or for his daughter-in-law Preeti whom he succinctly describes as "Pretty, charming, graceful and sly as a snake," and sums her up as a girl who "has an eye on my money." In course of the scene, we learn that Hasmukh is a diabetic and cardiac patient with a history of "high blood pressure, high cholesterol . . . (and] an enlarged heart." And all this goes towards explaining why towards the end of the first scene, he dies in bed where his wife discovers his dead body a few minutes later.

This is not the beginning of a tragedy however, for Hasmukh's ghost lingers on in the house, wandering through its walls (and occasionally sitting cross-legged on the dining table) keeping on passing acerbic comments on the actions and attitudes of the other (living) characters, though unheard by, and invisible to, them. Comically, even a member of the audience is not spared Hasmukh's ghost's not-so-veiled criticism, for at one point soon after he has passed away and assumed the role of a mock-chorus, his ghost sprawls on the dining table and dangles head and arms over its edge in imitation of swinging upside down from a tamarind tree, and points to a spectator in the auditorium and tells him sternly: "Your shoes need polishing!"

The central issue of the comedy—its complication—however emerges in its second scene in which it is revealed that none of his expectant family members have inherited his money, for what Hasmukh Mehta has done is to form a Trust to be administered over by his former mistress Kiran Jhaveri as the Trustee. In fact, according to the terms of Mehta's will, not only will his son not inherit his father's money and property until he is forty-five, but he will also have to compulsorily attend office everyday from 9 to 6 and remain under the official tutelage of Mrs. Jhaveri. And finally and most insulting to all the members of the family, Mehta's will stipulates that his former mistress will move in and live in his family till the Trust be dissolved twenty-two years hence.

All this points to the thesis of the play, which is the patriarchal dominance of Hasmukh Mehta both in the course of his life and after. As Ajit confesses after his father's death, "Ever since I was a little boy, you have been running my life. Do this, do that or don't do that, do this. Was I scared of you!" Or as Preeti, the daughter-in-law, tells Ajit, "He was a slave driver, your father! He almost drove me mad with his bossy nature. He succeeded with your mother." Even Kiran, the man's mistress, confesses to his wife at a candid moment: "He was so insensitive to other people's needs . . . yes, Mrs. Mehta. My father, your husband—they were weak men with false strength . . . will the scars our parents lay on us remain forever?"

The truth that emerges finally is that Hasmukh Mehta had wanted his son to live in his own image, just as he had lived his own life in thrall to his father's shadow:

Kiran: I should have hated him. Like I should have hated my father, my brothers and my husband. But all I felt for him was pity.

Hasmukh: (*As a ghost*) Enough: I say, enough! I paid you to do my work. Not ridicule me!

Kiran: Even his attempts at ruling over you after his death, through his will, are pathetic. (*Hasmukh sticks his fingers into his ears and shuts his eyes*) The only reason he wanted to do that is because his father had ruled over his family. All his life he was being a good boy to his father.

Sonal: How little I knew him. If I had understood him when he was alive, I would have died laughing. (510)

It emerges too that Mrs. Sonal Mehta had lived her life under the total dominance of her sister Minal, who always "decided what we should wear, what games we should play" and "Even at my husband's funeral . . . sat beside me and told me when to cry." But the play is not yet over, for in a surprise twist at the end it is revealed that Preeti had actually hastened, if not caused, the death of her father-in-law. Kiran holds this truth against Preeti, not to blackmail her, but to achieve a proper comic resolution by which the wife bonds with the husband, and the family bonds with Kiran and the Ghost of Hasmukh leaves the house forever, each of the family members having discovered his or her own identity finally separate from Hasmukh's overwhelming self.

Where There is a Will is quite evidently a young man's play which shows fairly optimistically that there is a way by which men and women can find happiness on their own terms. The developments, twists and surprises in the action are not however not facilely based on contrivances of plotting alone but far more appropriately on human motivations and wills. Each of the characters also develops Ajit (or Aju as his mother fondly calls him) is first projected through his father's unsympathetic eyes as a mother's darling and an ineffectual nincompoop—an estimation which even his wife seems to share—but is then shown to have resisted and even won, in however infinitesimal a way, against his father in the battle of wills. Mrs. Mehta, who had lived and suffered so long under the dominance of her husband and her sister, is shown to come into her own at the end of the play. The selfish Preeti ultimately learns the lesson that "giving is more important than taking," while Kiran Jhaveri finds the happiness that had so long eluded her in her past existence as a business-executive-cum-mistress to a rich man and as daughter to a drunkard and as wife to another.

The liberation of all these characters from the stranglehold of their past is of course also the defeat of Hasmukh Mehta. This domineering husband, heavy father and tyrannical boss is gradually dwarfed and diminished to the point of insignificance. Of course he never quite loses our sympathy for he is given an engaging comic vitality and verve (both in the flesh as well as a spectre), but we cannot help being unused when we hear that his erstwhile family has made plans to cut down the tamarind tree in the garden—his last terrestrial haunt. The truth underlying the comedy is serious enough: the man who would rule over his family even after his death is exposed at the end to be what he really was—a comitragic weakling who had constantly quested for a father-substitute, a man who was rude to everyone because he was insecure himself, an unfaithful husband who didn't really want a mistress . . . [but] a woman who would father him."

The so-called "Thesis play" in which a well-made plot provides opportunities to the characters to interact and to illustrate through their relationships the dramatist's *idée* is of course as old as Ibsen. That Dattani draws upon and exploits the resources of this convention of theatrical art is manifest in the way Preeti's substitution of her vitamin pills in the bottle of her father-in-law's blood-pressure tablets is discovered through a series of logical steps. Preeti's frustration at not having inherited Hasmukh's money leads her to abuse her husband and subsequently to burst into tears. Ajit's concern about the well-being of his pregnant wife leads him to look for tranquillizers—and he comes upon his father's tablets in Preeti's vitamin-pill bottle. Preeti cleverly sends her husband away from the room before he can inspect the tablets and throws them away together with the bottle out of the window, only to see Kiran pick them up below. Ajit, still looking for the tranquillizers, finds the tablets his father used to take for his blood pressure (in reality Preeti's ineffectual vitamin pills) and leaves them on the dressing table in Hasmukh's (now Kiran's) bedroom. Later, Kiran comes across this bottle, compares its contents with the tablets in the bottle she had picked up, and deduces Preeti's deed of substitution. This is plotting *par excellence*, as neatly done as the plot of a detective story.

Yet, what adds a new freshness to the old way of the thesis play is the sparkle of the dialogues and the texture of its presentation. To cite an example, here is the dead Hasmukh contemplating his photograph, put up by his son in a "conspicuous place":

> What's this? A sandalwood garland? Don't I get fresh flowers everyday? When my father died, I used to put fresh flowers on his photograph everyday for a whole month before getting a sandalwood garland. I wonder what became of his photograph? It was much bigger than this one. I also had it touched up to make him look more . . . dignified. Of course, I don't need help in that department. Those cheeks are too hollow. The lips are too tight. (*Stares for a while, then to the audience, seriously*) I don't have such mean little eyes, do I? My father had. Thirty years of living in the city and he got mean little eyes. Now where did that photograph of his go? I had taken it down when the walls were repainted. It's locked up in some trunk somewhere, I suppose. (*Takes a final look at his picture*) So that's it. This is how the world will remember me. Until my son locks me up in a trunk. *(Turns to Ajit*) Then all that remains of me is (*points to Ajit*) that! (*Pause*) This calls for some fresh air. I think I'll go outside and swing on the tamarind tree. Upside down. Might clear my head. (*Exits through the main door*) (487-88)

The first thing that strikes one about this speech is that it possesses a typically Indian flavour in its references to fresh flowers, sandalwood, garland, trunk and tamarind tree. The rather typical carping of the urbanized and more materially successful son (even though dead) about a rustic *dehati* father comes out in the lines "I . . . had it touched up to make him look more . . . dignified" and "Thirty years of living in the city and he got mean little eyes." Some other dialogues in the play have an almost Wildean hue of wit, as in Kiran's "Useful. What a useless thing to be." But what is far more innovative and original on the part of Dattani as a dramatist is his use of the injected dialogues of Hasmukh which, through unheard by the other characters, introduce a further dimension of implication for the benefit of the audience:

Kiran: He was just like his father, wasn't he?
Hasmukh: No. I wasn't.

Sonal: Yes. He was.
Hasmukh: Don't contradict me, woman!
Kiran: The same bossy nature?
Sonal: (together) No!
Hasmukh: Yes!
Kiran: Did he ever disagree with his father!
Sonal: (together) No!
Hasmukh: Yes!
Kiran: Did he ever do anything at all without consulting his father first?
Sonal: (together) No, never!
Hasmukh: Yes, always! (509)

Superficially comic and evocative of laughter, this finitely embodies a kind of dialogic strategy in that we are privileged to hear two contradictory statements about the same person. Unlike the Bakhtinian model of the dialogic in which there exists "a plurality of independent and unmerged voices and consciousnesses, a genuine polyphony of fully valid voices,"[7] we are of course expected to empathize with Sonal here, to valorize her version over that of Hasmukh. The function here is, in other words, ironic. But the device of an apparition's dialogues accomplishing the irony is also an extension and a radical one—of the older tradition of having a character say something in an aside and then of showing him to do or say something contrary in the presence of other characters. In any case, Dattani's use of a visible/ invisible, audible/inaudible ghost significantly pushes back the accepted borders of naturalistic drama. And finally, again to Dattani's credit, there is the use of an unstressed symbolism as the baby's kicking in Preeti's womb being symbolic of the start of a fresh new life for all the living members of the Mehta family, and the banishment of Hasmukh's ghost being indicative of the exorcism of the past.

II

A completely different kind of play, much more dark, starkly serious and violent, is *Bravely Fought the Queen*. A powerful domestic tragedy, this play highlights the circumstance of a woman fighting against all the odds that the forces of patriarchy have piled up against her. This woman is of course the "Queen" referred to in title of the play, a title which in itself is an intertextual derivation sourced from a translation of a Hindi poem about the indomitable Rani of Jhansi. Only, Dolly Trivedi is a woman who has to fight a battle against a violent and unfaithful husband, and against a tyrannical mother-in-law who rules over her sons and daughters-in-law with the weapon of her wealth even from her paralytic bed. The technical accomplishments of Dattani in this play also deserve mention, for what we have here is an extremely suggestive utilization of the stage as a multilevel space in which time itself is correspondingly layered. The stage-set is conceived in such a way that the mother-in-law's bedroom is placed at a level higher than the rest of the stage. Some of the action of the play is enacted on this upper level, occasionally in flashback. But what is really innovative on the part of Dattani is that this space is not only used to locate and to focus on action that is conceptionally taking place elsewhere at the same time, but also features enactment that runs simultaneous to the action proceeding on the main stage level. The result is a complex theatrical experience on the part of the audience, a performance in which time frames are collapsed, settings telescoped, actions visually played off against each other in a sort of theatrical equivalent of the split-screen technique sometimes used in films and in television.

The play opens on the view of the plushly fashionable but ill-maintained living room of Jiten and Dolly Trivedi. The two focal points of this set on the mainstage level are a well-stocked bar situated upstage centre, and a music system on which is playing a Thumri as the play begins. The action starts with the arrival of an unexpected visitor—Lalitha—who says that she had been asked by Jiten Trivedi, the boss of her husband Sridhar, to meet Dolly that very evening. Immediately, thus, is one of the basic issues of the play broached—that of the lack of communication (and worse) between husband and wife, for not only was Dolly ignorant of Lalitha's visit, but she was actually getting ready to go out for the evening in the company of her husband, his brother Nitin, and his wife Alka who is also Dolly's younger sister. Lalitha, it gradually emerges, has came to Dolly (on the instructions of Dolly's husband) to discuss details about a masked ball to be held as an event-launch for Re Va Tee, "a new range of colour-coordinated nightware and underwear for women," the advertising account for which Lalitha's husband Sridhar is hoping to acquire for the agency jointly owned by the brothers Jiten and Nitin Trivedi. Then, as the play proceeds, we get to know a little more about Dolly—that her sister (Alka) lives next door in a house identical to her own, built by the two brothers "right in the middle of nowhere," that Baa, their old widowed and paralyzed mother-in-law lives with them by turns, and that Dolly has a daughter named Daksha who is evidently in a school away from home.

In the next sequence of action, the two conversing women are joined by Dolly's sister Alka who too clearly expects to be taken out for the evening, since she has dropped in all dressed and made-up for their planned outing. Alka, we notice, is an alcoholic who helps herself to liberal quantities of rum, and it is hinted further that the two sisters have a secret lover in Kanhaiya, the nineteen year-old grandson of a friend of the vacationing cook who stays in the servants' quarters outside the house, and who comes for clandestine trysts in the kitchen. A recurrent theme is Lalitha's obsession with bonsai, a sample of which (a tiny tree with miniscule fruits growing on it) she has brought as a present for Dolly. Also, there are significant references in Act I to Praful, the brother of the two sisters whom Baa keeps calling for, but whom Dolly and Alka regard differently, Dolly as a loving brother whom she misses, but Alka as a patriarchal tyrant who had burnt her hair on a lit stove to punish her for having been dropped off at home from school by a neighbour's son on his scooter. We also come to know of an incident that had taken place two years ago, when Alka, under the influence of alcohol, had asked her mother-in-law whether her two very different looking sons had the same father, and had been thrown out of the house. And finally in the first Act, we are also told of the presence of an old shrivelled-up beggar woman in the courtyard who just refuses to be driven away.

These several strands of action and insinuation make up the first Act of *Bravely Fought the Queen*. What emerges from Act is no clear-cut thrust of direction, but a mysterious and brooding concatenation of circumstance and implication. Entitled "The Women," this Act plays off the three Trivedi women—Baa, Dolly and Alka—with and against each other in the presence of a fourth woman, Lalitha, the outsider who represents a kind of normality which the other three do not possess. And the basic picture that emerges is that of an isolated woman, Dolly, locked in a loveless marriage with an uncaring husband and a slightly demented mother-in-law who constantly intrudes into her personal space with her insistent demands for attention, her compulsive ringing of a loud electric bell to call her daughter-in-law to her room.

Act II, titled "The Men," is set in Jiten and Nitin Trivedi's office. The characters featured here are quite literally the counterparts of the women we have already seen in Act I, being Dolly's husband Jiten, Alka's husband Nitin, and Lalitha's husband Sridhar. In a quite striking bit of theatrical business, Mahesh Dattani presents the action of this Act as if it were a replay of the same segment of time over which the events of Act I had unfolded, only with a different cast and a different location. We are privileged to witness, in other words, the action that had been playing out in the brothers' office during the same period of time their wives had been waiting for them at home. Hence, while in Act I we had heard Lalitha, Alka and Dolly's side of the telephone conversations they had had with their husbands in the office, in Act II we get to hear the men's words spoken during the calls. Having been given the opportunity of seeing the wives in their domestic sphere, we are now shown the men in their milieu, the workplace. Only, there is a feature common to both the locales—the presence of Baa in her higher-level room at the back of the stage. As and when this space is illuminated, we get to hear the words of the conversation the old lady had with Lalitha and her daughters-in-law in Act I. Also common to the settings of both Acts in the bar from which Jiten helps himself to drinks, and like Alka in the previous Act, gets more and more drunk as the night wears on.

Act II opens with Nitin going through the company's accounts, ruing the fact they are "Always in the red. No matter how much money we earn." His e!der brother Jiten, also present on stage from the beginning, comes across as belligerently indifferent about the fate of their business and as a boozer who can think only of borrowing a large sum of money from Praful, their brother-in-law, whom, incidentally, both the brothers appear to hate. It is Jiten too who prevaricates and stops Praful from meeting his sisters at their home, even if he would have liked to do so. Then, in later on-stage discussion it emerges that the Re Va Tee campaign has run into rough weather since the audio--visual advertisement conceived for it is rejected as "tasteless and degrading" by all the women it had been tested on and even by the Board of Directors of the manufactures. Jiten however threatens Sridhar with dismissal if he does not sell the ad and later, more drunk, goes to the extent of ordering Sridhar to pick up a prostitute for him. Then, in Sridhar s absence, he raises the issue of selling Baa's ancestral house, which we now hear from Nitin has been willed by their mother to Daksha, his daughter. Immediately, he pressurizes Nitin to throw out his wife, this time permanently, so that Baa will be pleased and sign the property away to her sons. And finally, Sridhar enters, and to him are given the last words of Act II, uttered about the prostitute he has brought for his boss:

Sridhar: (shouting) She's young and fresh! (*Under his breath*) And she is great. I had her on the back seat. You can have my leftovers. (291)

Just as Act I of *Bravely Fought the Queen* had shown up the cracks and fissures of tension underneath the facade of the well-regulated lives of two upper-middle-class women, so in Act II we are given an insight into the deeper emotions that seethe within the psyches of the men of the Trivedi family. Nitin's "sensual" description of his brother's near-violent encounter with an auto-rickshaw driver with a "strong black arm," his evident unease over Sridhar's having seen an auto-rickshaw parked outside the office, and his complaint to his brother about call girls, "Why did you say we both pick them up?"—all gesture towards the fact that all is not what appears to be, at least where he is concerned. Between the two brothers, Jiten comes across as both violent and given to unpredictable mood-swings. Nitin however appears to be more quiet and balanced, even if more submissive and weak as a person. Yet, it is Baa's character which is most interesting and revealing, for in a series of flash-backs is revealed her tragic past of having been married to a dominating and violent man who had not only prevented her from singing in public, but also used to beat her up regularly and ill-treat her sons. It is made clear too that Jiten has taken after his father, while Nitin is like Baa, in appearance at least. At the same time, we are given another insight into Baa's character when it is revealed through her dialogue with Alka that she has never quite let go of her sons, and rules over them still, Nitin in particular, to the extent of stopping him from having children.

Act III of the play, headed "Free for All!" is set in Dolly's living room once again. It is raining as the action starts, and we remember that (as Baa had said in the preceding Act) it had rained too on Baa's wedding day. In the room, the sisters talk about Kanhaiya, and Lalitha wonders if Daksha too "hits it off" with her mother's lover. Naina Devi's thumri is re-played on the stereo all over again, and Dolly tells Lalitha all about this "queen of thumri" who had dared to "sing love songs sung by whores," even though she was occasionally mistaken for one herself. The story of the singer reminds Lalitha of a poem she had learnt at school—a poem about the Rani of Jhansi, some lines of which had run: "we'd heard her praises sung so often,/ So bravely fought the Rani of Jhansi,/So bravely fought the manly queen." And immediately we are reminded of Baa who had been stopped from singing by her tyrannical husband, and of Dolly and Alka's mother who too had "tried to be a singer. When she was young."

The flow of conversation in this Act, of reminiscence and speculation, is broken however by Alka's impulsive desire to dance and to get wet in the rain outside. It is clear enough that this impulse has been triggered off in the drunken Alka's mind by her sister's teasing earlier in this Act:

Alka: Is it raining?
Dolly: Yes! come look
Alka: Why?
Dolly: Because you like the rain!
Alka: Do I?
Dolly: Of course you do. You love getting wet and having your sari cling to you. Your bra and choli showing. . . . And you love doing a filmi number in the rain.
Alka: No, I don't.
Dolly: (*laughs)* I was just teasing you.
Alka: (*gets up, looking a little dazed*) I think the last drink really got . . .

Later while really dancing in the courtyard, Alka slips and falls and gets all covered in mud, just as her brother-in-law and husband come back home with Sridhar in tow. What follows is Jiten's insistence that his brother tell his wife about their decision to throw her out, but Nitin, more sympathetic and gentle, refuses to do so right away. Alka reveals too that her brother Praful had phoned her, and that she knows that it was Jiten who had stopped him from coming to pay his sisters a visit. Next, from a sequence of dialogue exchanged between Baa and Nitin in her room on the upper level, we hear Nitin asking his mother: "Baa . . . will you give me the house if I send her back—for good this time?" But then the ghosts of the past intrude into the present as Nitin's "voice changes to a child's," and he regresses into infantility and hatred for his father who would not leave his mother alone.

Back in the main action of the drama, Alka gets more and more intoxicated, even as Dolly stands by her as a support, both literally and figuratively, and as Jiten insinuates that Alka must be having a secret love-affair with someone. And then as Alka exits to bed fantasizing about going to the ball dressed up like the Rani of Jhansi, Baa's area on stage is lit up again and we learn that Baa has nominated Praful to serve as the trustee to the property she has willed to Daksha. This revelation makes Nitin burst out in anger and indignation:

> What have I done to deserve this? Oh God! All my life I have listened to you and obeyed you. Only once I have gone against your wishes, and you punish me for that? But he is to blame. Praful tricked me into marrying her! If you want to hate anyone, hate him. I hate him now! Do what you want with the property but don't let him run my life! He's out to get us! Alka can stay here, or go away, or drink herself to death, I don't care. It doesn't make a difference to me! But get him out of my life! (305)

More complications follow in the action as Jiten insults Lalitha, and Sridhar fights Jiten over this. Lalitha notices an auto-rickshaw parked outside the house; and when Sridhar goes out to try and hire it to take them back to their home, she sees the auto-rickshaw driver climbing over the compound's wall. This surreptitious visitant she takes to be Kanhaiya's friend—and perhaps another of Dolly's secret lovers.

Jiten, having entered at this point from the kitchen where he had gone to fetch some ice, has a confrontation with his wife, now. Dolly cries out that in all her sixteen years of marriage, she had won out against her husband only once, and that was when she had become a mother. The revelations that fall out through both Dolly's anguished dialogues and through Baa's confessions at the other stage-level are that Praful had concealed from the Trivedis the fact that his and Dolly and Alka's mother had been (as Baa puts it) "a keep . . . a mistress . . . a whore," and that urged on by Baa, Jiten had beaten up his wife even when she was pregnant with Daksha. And finally, the shocking truth tumbles out that Daksha is no dancer at all, but a spastic child who had been born two months prematurely as the consequence of the beating Dolly had from Jiten.

The play does not end here, however, for Dolly's furious taunting outburst:

> No! oh no! I will not let you get away so easily!
> They were your hands hitting me! your feet kicking me!
> It's in your blood! It's in your blood to do bad.

literally forces Jiten to run out of the house and in an act of compulsive violence to run over the old beggar woman again and again with his car. On her part, Lalitha, convinced that Kanhaiya is waiting in the kitchen, enters that room only to be puzzled by the fact that no Kanhaiya actually exists. And finally, all the other characters having left the stage but for Alka who sleeps in a drunken stupor on the living room sofa, the last dialogue in the play, a kind of soliloquy or confessional monologue is delivered by Nitin in an address to his sleeping wife. And all the mystery is ultimately cleared up as we hear that Nitin is a homosexual who had fallen in love and had been seduced by Praful, and we watch him go out to the auto-rickshaw driver with the "Powerful arms" who waits for him in the outhouse.

III

At its most basic, *Bravely Fought the Queen* shows the distance in dramatic maturity travelled by Dattani from his early conceiving of the well-made play plot-structure in *Where There is a Will*. For instead of having a simple lay-out of exposition-complication-resolution, what we are confronted with in the later play is a far more complex piece of dramatic construction—a plot that conforms more to the structure of a crime thriller with all its jigsaw bits and pieces of information that make complete sense only in the light of the unexpected revelation made in the end. A re-reading of the text of Dattani's later play indeed shows how carefully plotted is the whole. In the first Act only, Dolly's evident confusion over the name and location of the school Daksha goes to, the real reason behind Alka's calling her brother a liar and a cheat, the sarcasm concealed behind Alka's comment, "She doesn't tell everyone that her daughter is training to be a dancer"—all these are layered ironies which become evident only in the light of what we come to know later.

Yet, technical innovations and dramaturgical accomplishments apart, *Bravely Fought the Queen* is also essentially a character-drama, or more specifically a play in which the characters are conjoined with ideological shadows which are themselves cast by such fundamentally societal functions as patriarchy and the will to dominate. In fact, in one way the thesis of this play is somewhat similar to that of *Where There is a Will*. As Hasmukh had been his father's son down to possessing his father's mean little eyes, so too does Jiten in *Bravely Fought the Queen* resemble his father in appearance and in nature. Both Hasmukh and Jiten, together with Praful in a different key, represent the darkest face of patriarchy—intolerance, hatred, dominance—passions all fuelled by inner insecurities and complexes of guilt and fear. Praful is perhaps the worst offender in this respect, for there is more than a tinge of sadism manifest in his action of deliberately lighting a stove before pushing Alka's face close to the flames so that her hair caught fire, and in his making of Nitin ashamed of himself after every act of sex with him, and in his tricking of both Alka and Nitin to get married while keeping them in the dark about each other's sexual orientation.

Of course the fall-out of patriarchy taints the women in this play too. Baa, the physically and emotionally abused woman, is reactionally led to reject the son who resembles her husband and to possess the one who looks like herself and to alienate him from his father. And while the play does not say this in so many words, it is clear enough that it is this Oedipal instinct that drives Nitin into the arms of men who are father-figures to him—like Praful or like the auto-rickshaw driver with his black, powerful arms. It is the heavy weight of patriarchy too which turns Alka into an alcoholic, and which heaps defeat after defeat on Dolly. Only, Dolly is a Rani Jhansi in her own right—a fighter capable of confronting and humbling the patriarchal man who would run her life for her and deny her the slightest liberties and love that is her due as a woman, wife and mother.

In a way, through Dolly whose very name betrays the role and identity a male-dominated society would fain impose on her, and through Nitin who embodies the so-called "feminine" instincts of love and sympathy and understanding and tenderness, Dattani's play challenges society's stereotypical constitutions of male and female identity. The locus of this awareness is sited in the phrase about the Rani of Jhansi: "Bravely fought the *manly* queen. The implication contained herein is that a woman has to be "manly"—that is, conform to the construction of manliness as propagated by patriarchy—in order to be recognized as brave. But in the inset story of Naina Devi we are presented with another, divergent, paradigm of heroism. This is that of a woman motivated enough to do what she wanted to do even in the face of patriarchal opposition that would brand her a "tawaif" or whore, a woman who ultimately was acknowledged to be a queen by dint of her resistant will.

A little more free in her relationship with her husband is Lalitha who is "liberated" enough to enjoy the "not-so-occasional" drink, and "to do exactly the opposite of what [her] husband want[s]" but is not capable for all that to go home without her husband as an escort. Lalitha who "write[s] an occasional woman's column for the Times," sometimes "review[s] cultural events" and is also "into meditation" represents the educated Indian married woman without a full-time profession or office job. Childless by choice (her husband and she are saving up to buy a flat), Lalitha's passion for growing bonsai is symbolically reflective of her own mindset. The wiring and trimming she subjects growing plants to may well be what she has done to her own life: control and restriction. The result may be quaint and attractive, but it can also become ugly and grotesque like the bonsai Sridhar keeps on his office table, and which, additionally, is a clear symbol of the deformed relationship the brothers have with their wives.

Equally apt and telling are the other smaller symbols in the play. Dolly's facemask, which she is careful not to crack by laughing but which nevertheless cracks a little later, is one such symbol. Functionally, it represents the image of normality as housewife, daughter-in-law and mother which she presents before Lalitha and the world in the opening pages of the play, but which cracks open as the dark secrets in her life tumble out. The beggar-woman represents the guilt-laden burden of the past which Jiten would destroy if he could. Baa's wheelchair, never used in the course of the play, perhaps signals more than her paralytic condition. The thumris of Naina Devi played over and over again on the stereo-system simultaneously evoke and comment on the yearning for love and fulfillment experienced by all the major characters in the play. But by far the most potent symbol in *Bravely Fought the Queen* is a non-existent one—the fantasy of Kanhaiya who is both present and not present in the empty space beyond the kitchen door, like Radha's eternally young lover in Indian mythology who is forever available to the believer whenever she wills him into existence and being.

Certainly the more prosaically inclined Lalitha can never understand this. But we as spectators sympathetic to the frustrations, sufferings and trauma of Dolly and Alka Trivedi do, and so we empathize with their need to make the fiction they create. In this way too does Mahesh Dattani's play transcend its function as a performance script pure and simple and become a living and significant work of art, evoking in our minds an intellectual response even as it engages our emotions and feelings.

NOTES

1. Girish Karnad, Author's Introduction, *Three Plays* (New Delhi: Oxford University Press, 1994), p. 11.
2. *Ibid.*, p. 12.
3. A.K. Ramanujan, "Introduction," *Folktales from India* (New Delhi: Viking, 1993), p. xiii.
4. Girish Karnad, *Naga-Mandala*, *Three Plays*, p. 27.
5. John McRae, "A Note on the Play," *On a Muggy Night in Mumbai*, in *Mahesh Dattani: Collected Plays* (New Delhi: Penguin India, 2000), p. 45.
6. Mahesh Dattani, *On a Muggy Night in Mumbai*, Act I, p. 49.
7. Bernard Shaw, qtd. Christopher Innes, *Modern British Drama 1890-1990* (Cambridge: Cambridge University Press, 1992), p. 21.
8. Michael Walling, "A Note on the Play," *Bravely Fought the Queen*, in *Mahesh Dattani: Collected Plays*, p. 230.
9. Erin Mee, "A Note on the Play," *Tara*, in *Mahesh Dattani: Collected Plays*, p. 320.

The Thematic Thrust of Dattani's *Final Solutions*

S.S. SHARMA
IGNOU, New Delhi

First performed in Bangalore in 1993 Mahesh Dattani's play *Final Solutions* foregrounds the Hindu-Muslim problems. It also tackles the theme of transferred resentments in the context of family relations. The larger part of the play is good theatre and that makes it technically sound. The language is handled quite competently. Our present concern is with the play's thematic side. So let us focus on that.

Dattani has attempted a neat balancing act when it comes to tracing the malady of communal disharmony to certain elements within both the communities—Hindu and Muslim. The diagnosis offered is also sound enough. Paid people cause riots or politicians play upon the susceptibilities of the two communities on certain key issues. The chorus is a good device to express the broad way in which the thinking of excitable elements within the two communities goes. Processions being taken out and then attacked and then retaliation. Somebody there always is who throws the first stone. Food habits or kitchen-fads of the two communities are brought into focus. Utensils getting contaminated by the touch of a member of the other community is one such fad.

Then there are resentments within the family of Ramnik Gandhi. Smita feels stifled at home.

> Aruna: Does being a Hindu stifle you?
> Smita: No, living with one does.

Smita sees a lot wrong with the way Aruna is. Aruna's husband is also on the disapproving side. He has an exchange with Javed but neither is much wiser as a result. Bobby (Babban) tries to de-fuse things all the time. At a time there was something between him and Smita. Smita already knows Javed and Bobby when they seek shelter after being hounded by a mob. She knows Javed's sister Tasneem also. She also knows what Javed does. This is the unraveling part of the plot.

The other unraveling is about the shop that got burnt down. That accounts for a guilt feeling. So self-righteousness wouldn't do. Smita feels stifled by Aruna but would not like her father to use Aruna's ways as a way of dominating her. There she is on Aruna's side. When Ramnik asks her why she didn't tell him how she felt, her reply is that she didn't want to tell him because that would have been a triumph for him over Aruna. She says:

> How easy it would have been for us to join forces and make her feel she was wrong (386)

One of the climactic scenes in the play is when Bobby touches Krishna's idol. He says that Krishna smiles at our trivial pride and trivial shows. To Javed he says;

> See Javed! He doesn't humiliate you. He doesn't cringe from my touch. He welcomes the warmth of my hand. (400)

To everybody in general he says: "And if you are willing to forget, I am willing to tolerate." (400) He sees himself as a human being who believes, and tolerates, and respects what other human beings believe. The other climactic moment comes in the form of Ramnik's confession to Hardika:

> It's their shop. It's the same burnt up shop we fought from them, at half its value. And we burnt it. Your husband. My father. And his father. They had burnt it in the name of communal hatred. Because we wanted a shop. (401)

There is a 'Director's Note' from Alyque Padamsee appended to the play. In it, Padamsee says: "The mob in the play to is symbolic of our own hatred and paranoia. Each member of the mob is an individual yet they meld into one seething whole as soon as politicians play on their fears and anxieties." (403)

The fears and anxieties of the two communities are partly an aftermath of partition. Then there is the feeling of being second-grade citizens. There is the sensitivity to music being played near a mosque. There is the Hindu sensitivity in the matter of general Muslim food habits that go against vegetarianism. There are fears of contamination. Politicians exploit most of these things and hired goons help them. Saner voices like Bobby's are drowned, ignored or brushed aside. Pent up feelings take a violent shape.

As far as the Ramnik Gandhi family goes, it is a lot like Pinter's play *Homecoming*. Everyone wants his/her own space but something keeps simmering. Secrets tumble out under pressure. Unconscious and conscious fears and prejudices rule. Quite a few kinds of liberalism are often only skin deep but these are needed nevertheless. Collectively a lot of healing needs to be done. Better education and greater mixing would be a part of the answer.

Crisis situations bring out both our better parts and our worse parts. We can be quite cruel as a collectivity and (with the best of intentions) can be touchy for all the wrong reasons. All of us have the basest emotions hidden inside us. A demon lurks all the time. We all look for scapegoats. The false feeling of superiority is perhaps one of the worst things in such situations.

Dattani conveys all this—and more—dramatically. He allows his characters room to develop. He has a good theatre-sense and his command of language is good. He often takes up tricky issues and is able to bring a lot of equanimity to his handling of these. The dialogue is mostly crisp. Character-contrasts work well. He is able to delve deep into the unconscious levels of community thinking and brings a lot of objectivity and balance to his analysis of the problems that bedevil us.

When it comes to the film version of the play, the tilt perhaps is too much to one side. That possibly was reason for some other problems the film version had with the censors. Now that has been sorted out but one can't help feeling that greater objectivity, sensitivity and pragmatism is needed when transferring such issues to the film.

Mahesh Dattani's *Final Solutions*: A Play about Transferred Resentments

SATISH BARBUDDHE
Achalpur City

In 1998, Mahesh Dattani won the Sahitya Akademi award for his *Final Solutions and Other Plays*, published by East-West Books, Chennai, thus becoming the first English language playwright to win the award. His plays have been staged to critical and public acclaim all over the country and abroad. Mahesh Dattani has completely transformed the face of urban theatre in India.

Final Solutions is a stage play in three acts. The play was first performed at Guru Nanak Bhavan, Bangalore, on 10 July 1993. The play was also translated into Hindi by Shahid Anwar and directed by Arvind Gaur for Asmita Theatre in 1998. The play was performed at Tara Theatre, Mumbai, on 11 December 1993, directed by Alyque Padamsee.

Most of us experience anger in some form or other almost every day. Anger is a negative emotion; it can cause violence, it can ruin relationships. When a person is angry, he tries to take out his/her anger on anybody closest to him. Alyque Padamsee writes in "A Note on the Play": "Taking out your anger on your wife, children or servants is an old Indian custom."[1]

The characters in the play motivate us to think that angry outbursts lead to chain reactions. The play opens with Daksha reading from her diary. An oil lamp converted to an electric one suggests that the period is the late 1940s. Daksha is the grandmother of the Gandhis, who sometimes is seen as a girl of fifteen on the stage. Daksha thinks that she is "a young girl who does not matter to anyone outside her home." (166) She says: "Last year in August, a terrible thing happened . . . and that was freedom for India." The Mob whispers: "Freedom! At last Freedom!" Daksha closes her diary and now Hardika appears on the stage. She feels the things have not changed that much. A period of forty years is not a long period for a nation. But on the stage, the drumbeat grows louder and the Chorus slowly wear the Hindu masks. The words spoken by Chorus show the beginning of disharmony and painful period ahead. As long as the persons are on the stage they are normal but as soon as they are behind the masks, their thirst for blood rises. Whether we are angry with someone or someone is angry with us, each outburst takes its toll on both parties. The Chorus with Hindu masks burst with angry words:

Chorus 1: The procession has passed through these lanes
Every year,
For forty years!
Chorus 2, 3: How dare they?
Chorus 1, 2, 3: For forty years our chariot has moved through their mohallas.
Chorus 4, 5: What did they?
Why did they today?
Chorus 1: How dare they?
Chorus 2, 3: They broke our rath.
They broke our chariot
and felled our Gods!
Chorus 1, 2, 3: This is our land!
How dare they?
Chorus 1: It is in their blood!
Chorus 2, 3: It is in their blood
to destroy!
Chorus 4: Why should they?
Chorus 5: It could have been an accident.
Chorus 2: The stone that hit our God
was no accident!
Chorus 3: The knife that slit the poojari's stomach
was no accident!
Chorus 4, 5: Why should they?
It could have been an accident. (168)

The words spoken by Chorus are the indications of domestic violence, political mischiefs and social unrest. The effective use of the Chorus in the play is a dynamic technique used by the playwright. In the stage directions, the playwright gives hints on the Mob/Chorus.

> The Mob/Chorus comprises five men and ten masks on sticks. The masks are strewn all over the ramp. The player 'wears' a mask by holding the stick in front of him. At more dynamic moments, he can use it as a weapon in a stylized fashion. There are five Hindu masks and five Muslim masks. The Mob/Chorus become the Chorus when they 'wear' either the Hindu or the Muslim masks. But when referred to individually, they remain Chorus 1, Chorus 2, etc. The players of the Mob/Chorus do not belong to any religion and ideally should wear black. (165)

"Their chariot fell in our street!" remarks Chorus 1 with Muslim masks. The words 'This is our land,' 'fell in our street' show that the borderline is clear. Nobody thinks it is the land of Indians. Hardika says that the pride has destroyed her before. Her family doesn't want equality. It wants to prove superior than somebody else. Hardika can't stand this 'wretched' pride game.

In the living room of the Gandhis, Aruna, Ramnik Gandhi's wife, enters while Aruna's daughter Smita and her husband are retiring for the night. Ramnik doesn't like Hardika's telling his daughter that "those people are all demons." (173) Aruna is a typical Gujarati housewife doing 'pooja-path' everyday. She is overburdened by work. The following dialogue is a comment on the creator of the chaotic situation. When Aruna complains about her uneasiness, Ramnik asks:

Ramnik: Nobody is asking you to pray all day.
Aruna: Who do you think is protecting this house?
Ramnik: Who do you think is creating all this trouble? (173)

Aruna promises everybody: "Our Krishna will protect us." (174) Aruna is a God-fearing woman who thinks that everything will be smooth and peaceful one day. There is Lord Krishna who will protect everyone.

Daksha remembers her best friend Zarine. She admires her beauty: "I have never met anyone as pretty as her! What a complexion! It's true that Khoja women are the prettiest in the whole world." (175) Daksha feels her beauty but hates the place where she lives as it is "a place where they sell unmentionable things." (175)

Ramnik saves the two boys, Bobby and Javed, when the Chorus shout: "Kill the sons of swine!" It is the demon of hate that has been let loose. Nobody helps the boys. Finally, Ramnik opens the door for the boys. The bitter hatred intensifies. The irrational behaviour of the two communities lingers for some time showing one's prowess over the other. Chorus 1, 2 shout: "We are few! But we are strong!" (179)

Chorus calls Ramnik 'a traitor' for protecting the boys. Deep hatred makes the Chorus devoid of any human feelings. Hardika betrays her feelings by saying that she hates Javed. Aruna wants that the boys must go away from the house. She gives them water but puts the empty glasses separate from other glasses. Act I ends with the violent words of the Chorus: "Throw them out!" (187) The Chorus goes to the extent of saying: "You mad man! They'll stab you in the back! They'll rape your daughter." (186)

At the beginning of Act II, the characters are all in the same position as at the end of Act I. The Mob/Chorus is restless. The conflict deepens as the chariot lies broken in their streets. Chorus 1 doubts their leader's intentions. He says, "They want our blood to boil." (188) But what should boiling blood lead to, nobody knows. Chorus 1 laments that the leaders have succeeded in their mission. After lot of bloodshed and bitter enmity, the Chorus understand their flaw.

Smita recognizes the two boys as Javed, Tasneem's brother, and Babban or Bobby, Tasneem's fiancé. Tasneem is Smita's classmate. Smita's feeling of hatred for the political parties can be traced here:

Smita: (to Ramnik) They hire him! They hire such people!
Ramnik: They who?

Smita: Those—parties! They hire him! That's how he makes a living. They bring him and many more to the city to create riots. To . . . throw the first stone! (195)

Javed turns furious at these words and calls Smita a "Traitor." (195)

Act III opens with a spotlight on the two men sitting on the floor, looking troubled. The Muslim Chorus is on the highest level of the ramp. They sit with their legs folded under them in prayer position. The wordy duel between Ramnik and Javed goes on, accusing each other. The flames of hatred are still in their minds. Ramnik says to Javed that his life is based on violence. Ramnik thinks that Javed is a riot-rouser and criminal. Ramnik emits a few curses on Javed.

Ramnik thinks that Javed has done an unforgivable act. Ramnik, a liberal-minded person, offers a job to Javed only to give him a chance.

Daksha's complaint about her in-laws that they don't allow her to play gramophone makes Zarine sympathetic about Daksha. Zarine's father is busy narrating the stories about the clash between two communities and how his shop is burnt purposely. Javed sarcastically remarks: "You scream with pain and horror, but there is no one listening to you. Everyone is alone in their own cycles of joy and terror." (205) Javed admits that he himself doesn't know, what he is doing there. He is totally disillusioned. Smita frankly tells her mother, Aruna, not to burden her anymore with religious prejudices.

In the last lines of the Third Act, Bobby picks up the image of Krishna and tells everybody: "He does not burn me to ashes! He does not cry out from the heavens saying He has been contaminated!" (224) Aruna feels uneasy by seeing this act but Bobby clarifies: "if you are willing to forget, I am willing to tolerate." (225)

Ramnik transfers his anger at his own father's black deed (burning the shop) to his mother. In the name of communal hatred, this shameful act is done by Ramnik's father. This is the reason why he does not want to go to his shop. In the play Smita looks very innocent. She doesn't like hypocrisy or over-reaction to religious duties. So she openly opposes her mother: "I can see so clearly how wrong you are." (211) Aruna is proud of her religion. Aruna listens to the stories of Gods while Smita thinks it is all rubbish. Aruna's own daughter does not show any respect for all the religious rituals her mother observes. Smita boldly says to her mother: "You have to admit you are wrong." (210)

We have to oust anger from our lives if we want to live peacefully. Are there any final solutions to the problem of communal riots, disputes and acts of hatred? Can we come out of this vicious circle? Mahesh Dattani gives no answer. Alyque Padamsee asks: "Is life a forward journey or do we travel round in a circle, returning to our starting point?" (161)

The play is a fine example of transferred resentments. Smita, who is unable to express her love for Babban, criticizes her mother bitterly. Smita hates praying and fasting. Her mother accuses her of running away from religion. The characters in the play express their anger at every stage. The members of the raging communities do not know that negative emotions like anger tend to release harmful toxins in the body. The mob seems to be symbolic of our own hatred. We, the people of different communities, must stop this hatred and bitterness. The play mocks at the politicians who use people as their puppets. These puppeteers are the real culprits. The playwright, at the end of the play, wishes to stop this game of hatred and communal tension through the character of Ramnik. Ramnik accepts that his father has done the black deed. We should forgive the offenders and forget the past. This can be the final solution.

NOTE

1. Alyque Padamsee, "A Note on the Play," in Mahesh Dattani, *Final Solutions*, *Collected Plays* (New Delhi: Penguin India, 2000).

Contemporary Social Issues in the Plays of Mahesh Dattani

Rozario Ignatius
Scott Christian College, Nagercoil

Our country is passing through an ugly phase of 'contrariness.' The recent emphatic win of India over Pakistan in the current edition of the ICC Cricket World Cup 2003 vindicates this. The euphoria was definitely not an expression of unalloyed joy over India's cricket victory but something beyond. On the one hand, fireworks lit up the night sky with sweets being distributed and announcements of awards and concessions to the players who were earlier cursed and denounced but now glorified and deified. On the other hand, violence was unleashed creating a free-for-all situation with deaths reported and the injured being rushed to hospitals and the clamping of curfew. Both forms of ventilation of feelings border on madness. All these point to the truth: "The demons of communal hatred are not out on the street . . . they are lurking inside ourselves."[1] William Golding's phrase in *Lord of the Flies* 'the end of innocence, the darkness of man's heart' corroborates this further.

The well-known stage director Alyque Padamsee muses: "Can we shake off our prejudices or are they in our psyche like our genes? Will we ever be free or ever locked in combat . . . Arabs against Jews, whites against blacks, Hindus against Muslims? Are there any final solutions?' This is exactly what Mahesh Dattani attempts to do in his *Final Solutions*. *Final Solutions* examines the so-called liberal attitude to communalism. We can discern, in this play, the repulsive, frenzied, perfidious power of the perpetrators of such crimes. Dattani highlights the deep sense of futility of such bloody acts of violence. This play was staged by Bombay Theatre group. Doubtless, there is a reference to issues drawn from the 1992 riots in Bombay.

In this play two Muslim boys Javed and Bobby (Babban) take refuge in the house of a Hindu businessman, Ramnik Gandhi, while a communal riot rages outside. The agony and suffering of both the Hindus and the Muslims during the time of partition is still green in Hardika's (Ramnik's mother) memory. It is only towards the end of the play she is rudely shocked to learn from her own son the truth for the 'mysterious' bitterness between them and their Muslim friends. She quite innocently asks her son:

Hardika: Haven't you gone to your shop?
Ramnik: No.
Hardika: Why? It is late. Your workers will be waiting for you.
Ramnik: I can't go.
Hardika: Why not?
Ramnik: I just can't enter that shop any more. I can't bear thinking about it.
Hardika: What?
Ramnik: I didn't have the face to tell anyone. For me there's no getting off. No escape.
Hardika: What are you talking about? (*Looks at her with pity*) It's their shop. It's the same burnt-up shop we bought from them, at half its value. (*Pause*) And we burnt it. Your husband. My father. And his father. They had it burnt in the name of communal hatred. Because we wanted a shop. Also they learnt that . . . those people were planning to start a mill like our own. I can't take it any longer. I don't think I will be able to step into that shop again. . . .
Hardika: (*Crushed*) Why didn't you tell me? All these years.
Ramnik: You have to live with this shame only for a few years now.

"The roots of Hindu-Muslim animosity are explored in this play which is set in an atmosphere of communal violence—Religious beliefs are put under the microscope and popular myths are exploded. The unstated comment seems to be: every religion is inherently oppressive."[2]

Final Solutions is just one successful play by Mahesh Dattani that handles one such social reality. Dattani has to his credit many other plays that depict other social issues in a bold new light. Dattani's plays are at once expressive, informative, persuasive and refreshingly enriching. Before setting out to briefly review his other plays a brief introduction to the playwright will not be out of place in an article of this nature.

Mahesh Dattani, the celebrated playwright, film scriptwriter and film director presently lives in the leafy neighbourhood of Bangalore. By nature quite shy, he initially obtained a degree in Advertising and Marketing Management from St. Joseph's, Bangalore. He also thoroughly familiarized himself in the family business of Printing and Packaging. Then he turned to writing plays. In a span of ten years, he wrote eight plays. Some of them are: *Where There's a Will, Dance Like a Man, Tara, Bravely Fought the Queen, On a Muggy Night in Mumbai* and *Final Solutions.* Like Harold Pinter, he too wrote for the radio. *Do the Needful* is first in the series of radio plays. This play was commissioned by the BBC Radio 4 for India's 50th Independence Celebrations. *Seven Steps around the Fire* is his first detective play. His plays have been successfully staged all over the country and even abroad. He was an immediate success on the stage because he was well-versed in all aspects of stagecraft. In fact, he has a theatre group (Playpen) in Bangalore. He has the distinction of being the first Indian English playwright to win the Sahitya Akademi award for his work *Final Solutions and Other Plays* in 1988. His plays collectively constitute a diary of lives and views that are worthy of serious study.

Mahesh Dattani is one of the few leading Indian English dramatists. Other popular names in this genre are Gurcharan Das, Gieve Patel, Shashi Tharoor, Uma Parameswaran and Manjula Padmanabhan. The greatness of Dattani lies in the fact that he expresses himself easily and naturally in a voice loud and clear.

A reading of Mahesh Dattani's plays brings to the fore many burning issues that beset the post-Independence Indian society. A patient review of some of these social concerns will greatly help in understanding and appreciating both the playwright and his predominately middle-class characters. It can be stated that every one of these central thematic issues stem from the opposition between tradition and modernity in perception of matters relating to core human relationships like love, sex, marriage and even faith.

Gay relations—homosexuality—is one of the issues that figures prominently in some of his plays. *On a Muggy Night in Mumbai* deals with this sensitive subject. While the traditionalists consider such a relationship as something unnatural, obnoxious and even sacrilegious, the gays think otherwise. They are a happy and proud lot. They would even like to assert their true identity and sanctity. "The play presents a group of well-to-do homosexuals in Bombay, their changing mutual relationship, their revelations, their self-delusions and self-discoveries. Though they are all sailing in the same boat, each has his/her own oar to put in, his/her own flag to hoist. Kamlesh is weak and sensitive: Sharad is his exact opposite, with his jaunty nonchalance. Ed assumes a double identity, with Prakash as his second *avatar*. Bunny is true to the 'kindred point' of home and the Homo Den; he is a good husband at home and a very competent one in his bedroom, while he enjoys himself as a gay soul in the company of the initiated. Ranjit solves his problem by going abroad where he feels he will be more readily accepted; and Deepali is a militant lesbian, who declares, 'Every time I menstruate, I thank God I am a woman.' Totally free of guilt, she is strong and bold enough to strike Ed when he becomes violent. The wedding music heard constantly in the background in the final Act is an ironic commentary on the lives of these homosexuals for whom 'marriage' can only be a doubly dirty twice-four letter word.'[3] It must be noted that this is the least produced of Dattani's plays. The reason is that directors fight shy of its unusual subject. But Dattani went ahead with courage to direct a film *Mango Soufflé* based on this play.

In *Do the Needful*, Alpesh, a 'thirty-plus and divorced' gay Gujarati boy is forced to marrying a 'twenty-four and notorious' South Indian girl named Lata. Interestingly, Lata is in love with a married Muslim terrorist, Salim. But, both Alpesh and Lata hoodwink their parents (a microcosm of middle-class society) by pretending to put on a semblance of an ideal couple when the truth is that they choose to go their own ways. Naturally, the hypocrisy of such arranged hotchpotch marriages for 'convenience' stands exposed.

Discrimination against the girl child (a microcosm of the world of woman) is handled boldly by Dattani in his play, *Tara*. The play deals with the courage and strong will of a handicapped Siamese twin who could have survived but for her mother's unwise and preferential decision to give up the extra leg to her twin brother, Chandan. "Tara, a feisty girl who isn't given the opportunities given to her brother (although she may be smarter) eventually wastes away and dies. Chandan escapes to London, changes his name to Dan, and attempts to repress the guilt he feels over his sister's death by living without a personal history."

Gender identity is yet another theme that dominates the plays of Mahesh Dattani. *Dance like a Man* questions the propriety of a man of over-stepping his jurisdiction by taking to dancing, Bharatnatyam. He is ostracized for he chooses to dance like a woman though his dancing is a way of expressing his identity. The social bias against the art of dance among men is highlighted in this play. Jairaj, the protagonist is shown the door because he goes against the expressed wishes of his father in choosing to dance his way through life. This lands him in great difficulty; he finds it hard to eke out a living. Naturally, after his father's death he destroys all things that are dear to his father. He does not even spare the rose garden.

Bravely Fought the Queen questions the male and female roles in society. The Queen in the title refers to the famous Rani of Jhansi. But in this play Dattani depicts the plight of helpless women victims of male tyranny. With the delineation of Baa, he handles the mother-son relationship. Baa is the mother of Jiten and Niten. She is an invalid who has been ditched by her husband. Embittered that she is, she sets up her sons against their wives. This act of being vindictive because of an angry and sad past is seen in other plays of Dattani as well. Jiten beats his wife Dolly when she is in an advanced stage of pregnancy. This results in her child being born deformed. Niten is a homosexual and so his wife Alka has her own tale of woe to narrate. Dattani's treatment of this mother-son relationship takes on psychological overtones.

Seven Steps around the Fire deals with the suppression of the marginalized hijra community. Uma Rao's research on this ancient tribe brings into focus the hypocrisy and repression that 'the big shots' are capable of because they are beyond the reach of law. Again in this play we observe how the Police Officer refuses to subject himself to any medical examination to rule out the barrenness of his wife due to his impotency. This bias of squarely blaming the women for her barren state is another societal phenomenon that Dattani exposes.

In *Where There's a Will*, we meet characters drawn from two generations: the father and the mother in Hasmukh and Sonal Mehta, and Ajit their son and his wife Preeti. Hasmukh is not happy about the prodigal behaviour of his son and also with the vainglorious attitude of his wife, Sonal. What he expects is implicit obedience to him, as he practised it in his father's case. When things drift away from his control he thinks of a checkmate. He creates a trust and appoints his mistress Kiran Jhaveri its trustee. This move renders all the members of the family to the position of pensioners. Even after his death, Hasmukh haunts his house as a ghost. The evils of patriarchy take centrestage in this play. Dattani covertly asserts that where there is a will there is a way.

The danger of HIV/AIDS, like terrorism, is of global concern. Fully comprehending the fatal implications of its spread, Dattani wrote out the script for the film *Ek Alag Mausam* (*A Different Season*). The film is about a woman who is HIV positive and the traumatic experiences she undergoes—some of the worst moments of her life. Dattani sees life in this deadly disease when he stresses the need to show love when it is most needed. He strongly feels it would augur well for us if AIDS does not have to be about inevitable death, but rather about life and a celebration of it. He remarks about the storyline of the film: "It moves away from just being a film about AIDS. It is about human dignity and pride, that as a civilized society we do not have the right to break. Thematically, it is about the triumph of the human spirit. It is a love story; after all, romance is an evergreen theme, but it's about love at a time when you need it most."[4]

That Dattani is a talented director could be substantiated by his first directional venture on the silver screen *Mango Soufflé*. This film was released in Bangalore, Mumbai, Pune and New Delhi on February 28, 2003. "Screened at film festivals at Bangkok, Austin, and the Sydney Mardi Gras since August 2002, *Mango Soufflé* is the official Indian selection of the London gay and lesbian film festival. It is slated to be shown at Turin, Toronto, San Francisco and Tokyo."[5]

Thus, Mahesh Dattani through his plays focuses on many contemporary social issues. "I write for my milieu, for my time and place—middle-class and urban Indian. . . . My dramatic tensions arise from people who aspire to freedom from society. . . . I am not looking for something sensational, which audiences have never seen before . . . some subjects, which are under-explored, deserve their space. It's no use brushing them under the carpet. We have to understand the marginalised, including the gays. Each of us has a sense of isolation within given contexts. That's what makes us individual."[6] This playwright/film personality cannot be easily sidelined because of his contemporaneity. The greatness of Dattani lies in the fact that he is one who believes that theatre is an art with a function.

NOTES

1. Mahesh Dattani, *Collected Plays* (New Delhi: Penguin, 2000).
2. *Indian Review of Books*, 16 March 1998-15 April 1999.
3. M.K. Naik, "Cinderella Still: Recent Indian English Drama," *Littcrit*, Vol. 27, Number 1 and 2, June-December 2001.
4. *The New Indian Express*, Friday, October 15, 1999.
5. *The Hindu*, Sunday, March 9, 2003.
6. *Ibid.*

The Sensational Issues in the Plays of Mahesh Dattani

SANGEETA DAS
D.G. College, Kanpur

After reading the plays included in the anthology *Collected Plays* by Mahesh Dattani, I am filled with admiration for the man as he had the far sight of focusing on such issues which are sidled by the prominent writers of today. Mostly the writers are concentrated on the feministic issues of today—feminism being a hot topic of the century. Whereas Mahesh Dattani makes himself conspicuous by picking up such sensational issues of the society which we know and read now and then but refuse to acknowledge their existence amidst us.

Besides being the most controversial issues, their discussion at times becomes very embarrassing and is likely to be refuted by the society. But I personally feel that in order to critically judge and of course give an unprejudiced verdict, one has to face reality and look into one's face straight without hiding behind the false curtain of social dogmas. Mahesh Dattani's daredevil attitude towards society and its loopholes is surely commendable and has impressed me a lot. Such playwrights and their deep study of the false ego of our society will definitely do something to sieve the dirt out of our society and make it a better place for one and all. All the eight plays are different from each other in substance. Each of them deals with different hurdles in the path of a progressive society.

Seven Steps around the Fire is all about marriage of a beautiful hijra Kamla to a son of a wealthy government minister named Subbu. This shocking revelation culminated into the murder of Kamla. The society accepts a hijra for gracing the ceremonies of marriage and births but would not allow them to partake of such ceremonies. The author has ironically portrayed this aspect which would not have been given any heed, for any matter related to them is of no importance to anyone. The heart-rending story about a hijra murdered simply because she fell in love with Subbu, a young man having a status of importance in society, fills us with horror and sense of injustice. But do you think we would do anything to help the hijra community and allow them a place of recognition in society and deal with them with compassion. No, that cannot be done. We would stand aside like mute spectators and look down our nose at them who are considered lower than the low.

On a Muggy Night in Mumbai is a tragicomedy which deals with homosexuals. In the play, Sharad and Deepali though comfortable with each other have different ways of being gay. More stress is laid on the character of Kamlesh and Prakash who is also Ed and romances with Kamlesh's sister Kiran. Initially Kamlesh and Prakash were ardent lovers when Prakash suddenly turncoats and changes into Ed, wearing the garb of a handsome guy, head over heels in love with Kiran, who unfortunately happens to be Kamlesh's sister. Kamlesh playing the role of a humble lover resigns himself to the changed situation without complaining. Nevertheless, his sexual needs are fulfilled by Sharad, his friend. He shocks us a bit by stooping down to mating with a guard for which he is ashamed of himself. Prakash who had now changed to Ed suddenly emerges into the room and the scene to meet Kamlesh's sister and bumping into Kamlesh is revived of his earlier crush on Kamlesh. Nonetheless Prakash/Ed is ashamed of being a homosexual and tries to leave the place with Kiran as soon as possible, to escape the cynical eyes of the others who knew about his relationship with Kamlesh. Kiran is shown to having all compassion for the gay people and wishes they could marry for happiness of her brother who she knew was a homosexual. The irony of the whole story is that the poor girl did not know that the man to whom she was going to get married was a homosexual and an ex-lover of her brother. The revelation in the end comes as a shock to her. The whole story throws light on the growing homosexuality and its non-acceptance by the Indian society. At one stage, Kiran innocently remarks: 'I really wish they would allow gay people to marry' to which Ranjit cynically replies 'They do. Only not to the same sex.' This again is an upcoming burning issue of today which is dealt in an adept way by Mahesh Dattani. Every second person may be a homosexual but fear of ostracism restrains him from exposing himself. Through this play, Mahesh Dattani has tried to soften the society towards the gay and subtly tried to stir up compassion for this class.

Do the Needful is another play which deals with another phase of complex relationship. In this play, the dual problem of love and homosexuality is deftly handled. Lata, the female character, loves Salim a Muslim belonging to a separate community and above all is a terrorist. Their marriage being an impossible event, Lata resorts to an incompatible marriage with Alpesh, a homosexual, whose homosexuality proves to be a feasible cover-up for meeting their respectable lovers—Lata and Salim; Alpesh and Trilok. Throughout the play, we are taken aback by Lata's indifference and stubborn attitude towards her expectant parents and at the same time thwarted by Alpesh's placidity and indecision towards marriage. Though towards the end it is finally Lata who embarks upon putting forth her reluctance to marry Alpesh before him, it is only then that he tells her about his refusal on their marriage. We being Indians hold the institution of marriage with great esteem. Treatment of this great institution as a trifle contract to facilitate their selfish ends fills us with great distaste. Both Lata and Alpesh could see no way out of the marriage arranged by their parents and were not ready to give up their respective lovers, so they strike upon a halfway through, which was suitable to both of them. But the path which both of them choose is a default and desecrates the sanctity of marriage and can never be acceptable to our society. This play stirs the feeling of misgiving for the characters—Lata and Alpesh. Though such characters may be existing in our midst but such blatant disregard for a sanctuous ceremony fills us with horror. No sooner Lata and Alpesh marry than they decide how to deceive their family and go and meet their respective lovers.

Final Solutions is a play outwardly focused on Hindu-Muslim incompatibility but inwardly full of mutual disagreements amongst the family members. The clash between fanaticism of Hindus versus fanaticism of Muslims is highlighted. Lack of accommodation between the two communities and unacceptability gives rise to acrimony resulting in terrorism and anarchy. The play itself is a question mark on this age-old enmity between the two communities wondering if there would ever be a final solution to this endemic problem.

Love does not restrict itself to religion, caste and creed is evident from Smita's hidden love for Babban, one of the outsiders. Her mother Aruna, a staunch Hindu lady believing in purity and distaste for the other community, faces opposition from her daughter Smita, who is thwarted by her mother's indifference towards Babban.

The electrified atmosphere within the house amongst the family members who have personal grudges against each other for their own reasons, facilitate the rioters Bobby and Javed to thrive on them and consequently save themselves from being destroyed by the mob thirsting for their blood, outside the house. To the readers, Ramnik Gandhi would seem to be a brave man who fortified himself against the Hindu crowd who seemed hatred personified to save the two Muslim rioters, but it was all out of resentment for his father's black deeds which he wanted to vent upon his mother Hardika who was shocked by his attitude and terrified by the consequences of her son's stubbornness.

Much could not be achieved out of the good act put up by Ramnik Gandhi as the roots of hatred and unacceptability are deep-rooted and require time and untiring efforts on both the sides to root out the tree of hatred.

Bravely Fought the Queen is a play which deals with women from rich families who enjoy recreating themselves with beautifying themselves and indulging in vigorous shopping sprees, parties, balls etc. Basically they are highly disappointed and distraught ladies who try to find solace in such activities. Alka and Dolly are two such ladies who make untiring and useless effort to drown their sorrows in booze and sex. Alka who is a perfect alcoholic pours out her venom towards her husband and brother-in-law in a drunken state. Her thirst for freedom and mobility from constant confinement in the house is seen when she goes out into the rain and dances in the mud regardless of spoiling her expensive sari. Nitin is a homosexual and consequently is unable to satiate his wife's desire which is also a source of pain for Alka.

Nitin and Praful had sexual relationship between them and we learn at the latter half of the play from Nitin's conversation with his mother that Praful tricked him into marrying his sister, Alka. No wonder he had no attraction or concern for Alka which becomes obvious from the same piece of conversation where he further says that he did not care if Alka stayed there or left or drank herself to death. He is over-awed by the lengthening impact of Praful over his life. He is portrayed as a man of weak will who neither wanted to disappoint his brother Jiten by refusing to divorce his wife nor Praful by divorcing his sister. To add to this turmoil there was the property which Baa was not ready to give him because of her annoyance on his marrying Alka against her will.

Jiten on other hand is shown to be a cruel, imposing and most discourteous man who did not have the courtesy to talk politely to a lady. His rudeness to Lalitha, Sridhar's wife is an example to support this. Jiten's character is a stark contrast to Nitin's. Jiten maintains a simultaneous life with prostitutes, whom he entertains in his office. Any opposition from his accounts officer Shridhar is met with threat to his job. In a nutshell, in this play, Dattani depicts the bizarre picture of high-class society. The play's name *Bravely Fought the Queen* centres on Alka who fights with Jiten right on his face even in her drunken state. She even goes to the extent of calling Jiten a leech.

Tara is again a play in which Mahesh Dattani picks up an issue which is glaring in our society and itches an Indian female in every walk of life. The preference of a boy child over a girl child forms the infrastructure of the play. The girl may be more enterprising than the boy but what is the great deal in it, she nevertheless fails in the race of favour. Both the twins revel in their love for each other and adoration of their parents. Everything shatters into irretrievable pieces when they come to know about the manipulation of their separation by their mother and grand-father, Tara eventually dies and Chandan escapes to London to hide his guilt which he feels strangely over his sister's death. This issue is quite prevalent in India and whether it is an educated or uneducated family, inclination towards a male-child is blithering and consequently the rising graph of female infanticide is mind-boggling.

This play also enlightens us that no matter how much a girl outshines a boy, she will remain in the background and can never be given an advantageous position. It being a man's world and the reins being in their hands, it is very difficult for the woman to fight out her way. Women should cling to each other and in consolidation, fight out the stranglehold of the men. It becomes a source of pity when such characters as Tara's mother worsen the conditions. If she had not shown indulgence for the male-child and had done justice with her female-child then both the children would have happily flourished and established themselves in the world. It is really shocking to read that Bharati, being an educated mother, showed such shortsightedness. Such incidents do much to hamper the mission of female-upliftment in a male-dominating society. Mahesh Dattani has succeeded commendably to stir up the spirits of the readers to fortify themselves against any such biased measures in life.

Dance Like a Man is a Chennai based play where dance is an integral part of life. The characters in this play Jairaj, Ratna and their daughter Lata are dancers. Ratna believes that her daughter should soar to such heights which she could not achieve because of opposition from Jairaj's father Amritlal. She considers herself a failure and for this she blames Jairaj. She vents her frustration on Jairaj and accuses him of being a jelly in front of his dominating father.

The impact of patriarchal authority in a joint family and kowtowing of the rest of the family members before their decisions has been specifically spotlighted in this play by Mahesh Dattani. Though now-a-days, nuclear families have become more prevalent in India, traces of joint families could still be found. The result of such high-handedness is quite natural as in the play. No sooner did Amritlal close his eyes than Jairaj changed absolutely starting by alteration in the house. Too much of stringency leads to revolt which, though remains undercover, gushes forth whenever it finds an outlet.

Where There's a Will is another play in which Mahesh Dattani has depicted another aspect of patriarchal dominance. Let it be daughter, wife, daughter-in-law or mistress, all are dependent on man for financial and physical security. Man has always taken up woman as a liability and a source of requirement. Women have been looked down upon by men as an object to meet their needs. They should be there to cook their food, smile cordially at his friends, run around attending to their needs and sexually satisfy them whenever they have the urge. If the wife is unable to satisfy the husband then there is always a mistress to do that. That mistress also is subject to compulsion to kowtow before him for he may be having reins to her weaknesses. Everything finally boils down to one conclusion, which is the autocratic nature of man discreetly dealt with by Dattani in this play. Hasmukh Mehta is an autocrat and cynical man who always criticizes his son and wife and also looks askance at his daughter-in-law. To him they are all his enemies trying to squander away his hard earned money. He also had a mistress name Kiran Jhaveri about whom he had a high opinion and had made the trustee of his property. His family was ignorant about his second relationship and its revelation was shocking to them which came their way after his death. But here the difference between a man and woman has been discreetly outlined by Dattani. Hasmukh being a man was arrogant and tactless and therefore was unable to make place in the hearts of his family members, whereas Kiran Jhaveri being his mistress, had impressed Sonal so much that she became her confidante. Ajit and Preeti also accepted her as one of them and were quite at ease with her. Hasmukh Mehta, whose spirit was a mute-watcher of all the developments in his house after his death was greatly disappointed and thwarted to see his mistress take the place amongst his family members which he had desired throughout his life.

The various plays written by Mahesh Dattani and enacted in different theatres of the country and felicitated world-wide, gives us a glimpse into such hidden issues that have been existing and unconsciously accepted by us. But such issues have never been given so much importance as to find their way into print. To pull them out from under the rug and display them threadbare is an uphill task and requires grit and forbearance which Dattani has proved that he has.

Diversity of Themes: The Plays by Mahesh Dattani

ALKA TYAGI
Dyal Singh (E) College, University of Delhi

Indian English drama has been thriving on translations and adaptations as far as serious substantial theatre is concerned. And the whole spectacle of Indian English stage fades into insignificance if it is not for a few names like Mahesh Dattani. Dattani is one of the most significant contemporary playwrights writing in English. His plays artfully touch some of the most serious concerns of our society today.

'Naturalism' is the expression that comes to mind when one reflects on the plays of Mahesh Dattani. The subjects of his plays not only reflect life but they deal with life head on. Gay-relations, communal violence, human relations and the ordinary, untouched, unthought conflicts between son and father, husband and wife, lovers etc. are tackled with a skilled frankness. That Mahesh Dattani is a successful playwright is no more a contested issue. His art is revealed in his rendering of contemporary social problems in a manner that is unique to him. His characters are fully rounded men and women, and gays with a past behind them. The character's psyche is revealed through their dialogues which offer a plane for the dramatist to display his wisdom and wit as well as his humour. Themes of some of his plays are discussed in the following section.

Seven Steps around the Fire is a very modern play about the ancient mystery of a whole tribe. Uma Rao is writing her thesis on the origin and contemporary status of the 'Hijra community.' Her genuine (re)search for truth bears fruit by her sheer effort and will. Yet she is not powerful enough, in spite of being the daughter-in-law of a deputy commissioner and the wife of a superintendent of police, to bring this truth to light: Kamala, a beautiful Hijra, is murdered on a minister's orders and Subbu, Kamala's lover and the minister's son, commits suicide. Both the incidents are hushed up and the real culprit remains omnipotent and beyond reach.

On a Muggy Night in Mumbai is a play with a theme often not touched upon—gay relationship and their need to assert their true identity in society. Dattani deals with a difficult subject with a bold pen and lays open the hypocrisies of social life which imposes stereotypical roles to men and women and acknowledges and legitimizes only these roles. Male and female—these are the only sexual categories which have secured social existence and society's approbation. People who do not fit into these two classes either keep trying to fit into the rut and suffer throughout their lives a burden of living the big lie, or if they choose to live with the truth they have to bear social ostracism and contempt. With a fine delineation of characters like Ed and Bunny and Sharad and Kamlesh in a lively and witty manner, Dattani brings out the psychological pressures and fears, the real and the imaginary, gays have to live with. Dattani uses symbolic means to foreground his idea of gay relations. Kamlesh's small flat is a place where this gay group can meet openly. But in contrast to this small space available to them are visible and invisible signs of the outside world which has a continuous imposing presence—the Mumbai skyline, the wedding procession with all its loud paraphernalia, the beautiful woman who weeps and the failed air conditioner etc.

Do the Needful is about two upper class families which do not understand their children's desires and want to marry them against their wishes. The children, a gay Gujarati boy and a South Indian girl who loves a Muslim boy, cleverly clinch the deal between their parents, get married and under the cover of a traditional happy married couple go their own ways. Alpesh can carry on his affairs with Trilok and Lata can meet Salim whenever she wants to. Both keep each other's secret. It is again about social restraints against gays and against the social inhibition of inter-caste marriage. Lata and Alpesh refreshingly come as honest, young people of the new generation who are frank and open with each other at least.

Bravely Fought the Queen is a play about sinners and their secret guilts; it is about violence against women, about exploitation of the weaker, about the mean, squalid corporate world. The play seems to be approving Freud's theory about repression. Jiten, who had a very bad childhood has turned into a demon of a man. He is a violent, alcoholic, lecherous wife-beater inclined to kill at the slightest provocation. Nitin, who is a gay, is duped by his own best friend and suffers a guilt-ridden relationship with his wife Alka. The women—Baa, Dolly and Alka—are all victims of male anger. Dolly, beaten by Jiten while she is pregnant, delivers prematurely and consequently the child is mentally retarded. Alka, who longs for her brother Praful's acceptance of herself, silently suffers a fruitless marriage with Nitin. Shadows of the past are felt throughout the present and since past can't be undone there seems to be no end to it. The play doesn't even end formally. Here is a remarkable merging of content and form.

Deep down under a comedy are the most intense elements of a tragedy. *Where There is a Will* is one such comedy where Hasmukh, a self-made millionaire, wants to control the lives of his son, his wife and his daughter-in-law. His house is a battleground of arguments and counter-arguments between him and his wife and son. The daughter-in-law is too clever to offer defence. Hasmukh dies with a will to reform everyone. This psychic will of mind mingles with the legal document that he bequeaths as his will. The document holds the powers to control others now that he is dead. Atrocities imposed by the will are nothing compared to the heinous desires of the survivours for Hasmukh's money. *Where There is a Will* uses 'Will' as a fantastic pun.

Tara is about the courage and spirit of a handicapped Siamese twin who could have survived but for her mother's decision to give the extra leg to her twin brother. Roop's joke about how the Gujarati is used to drown their infant daughters in the milk comes out to be true in the end. Tara's mother got a leg amputated from her Siamese twins when there was a great probability of the survival of the girl.

Final Solutions is a very serious and delicate drama on the well-worn subject of Partition, the violence it unleashed and its after-effects which are still reflected in the communal riots that often arise. Dattani, however, is successful in touching the deep sense of futility which fills the heart of those involved in committing such violence. Javed is not the only sinner. Ramnik, Aruna and Hardika—all have played their part and ultimately have to share the burden of guilt. The final solution seems to be a life proposed by the young Smita and Bobby who posses a consciousness that is liberated from sifting caves of religious cults and who meet their fellow beings at a secular plane.

In most of Dattani's plays the past is a constant presence in the character's consciousness; mostly past is relived in the memory or narrated in the dialogue of characters. Old people are there in every play. They are neither stereotypically revered, morally perfect beings nor downright victimized beings. They are normal human beings with very real shortcomings and vices and virtues. In fact they are the carriers of the past with which they interact or cleanse the minds of the progeny.

Mahesh Dattani is a leading professional playwright for whom theatre is an art with a function. In all, his plays are a refreshing treat for a reader as his performances are to spectators with the innovative use of theatrical space and other elements.

Mahesh Dattani's *Final Solutions and Other Plays*: A Living Dramatic Experience

REENA MITRA
Christ Church College, Kanpur

Indian English literature, G.N. Devy points out,[1] is not one of the condescendingly designated "New Literatures" for it cannot adequately and comprehensively be defined as merely "postcolonial" in the sense that African and West Indian literatures can. Not only is there a two hundred year history of Indians writing in English but also a significant bulk of Indian writing that endorses any literary culture that is truly Indian. All Indian literature, including Indian English literature, represents the typically complex Indian experience which is historically multilingual and multicultural but does not fail to underscore well-defined concepts of national identity. Indian English literature has steadily moved towards self-assertion and self-definition and acquired an unmistakable sense of "selfhood."[2]

The origin of Indian drama can be traced back to the Vedic period. As a manifestation of our national sensibility Indian drama came into existence as a means of exploring and communicating the truth of things and was popularly hailed as the "Fifth Veda."[3] Iyengar, defining the scope of Indian drama said that it was envisioned to "comprehend the whole arc of life, ranging from the material to the spiritual, the phenomenal to the transcendent and provide at once, relaxation and entertainment, instruction and illumination."[4]

Bharata's *Natyashastra* in Sanskrit discusses the minutiae of ancient stagecraft and displays consciousness of all major aspects of drama, namely, stage-setting, music, plot-construction, characterization, dialogue and acting. Sanskrit drama flourished under the patronage of the court till the twelfth century but gradually ceased to be performed on the stage and entered a period of decadence which led to its virtual extinction. What replaced it was the theatre of the people and music, dance and drama was witnessed in varying forms. The "jatras" of Bengal, the folk plays of Tamil Nadu like *Satharam*, the "yakshaganas" of Andhra and Karnataka, the "kathakali" of Kerala, the "kirtaniya" of Mithila, the "Bhavai" of Gujarat and the Ramlila plays of North India—all these forms of entertainment had little value as literature but were characteristic of Indian culture, and represented a transition from the classical Sanskrit drama to the modern Indian drama. By 1920, a new drama in almost all the Indian languages came to the fore, it was a drama largely influenced by prevailing movements like Marxism, psychoanalysis, symbolism and surrealism.

For certain reasons which need to be identified, the development of Indian English drama has not been able to keep pace with that of poetry and fiction. The theatre movement in English has always trailed along far behind the flourishing prevalence of Indian poetry and fiction in the same language. It was as early as 1871 that Michael Madhusudan Dutt wrote the first Indian play in English, *Is This Civilization?* There was, however, no follow-up creative dramatic activity for years, one reason, perhaps, being that the total commitment required on the part of the playwright, the actor and the audience could never really be coordinated for a living dramatic experience. Also, it is difficult to lend conviction to a dialogue in English between two Indians who normally converse in their mother tongue. The difficulties, however, have been overcome by many and the pre-Independence era saw the emergence of literary giants like Rabindra Nath Tagore, Sri Aurobindo, T.P. Kailasam, Harindranath Chattopadhyaya and Bharathi Sarabhai, who, through their plays, gave a fillip to the growth and development of Indian English drama and opened up new vistas in the genre. This pre-Independence crop of dramatists, despite the poetic excellence, thematic variety, technical competence and symbolic and moral significance of their works, did not give enough weightage to the actability and "stageworthiness"[5] of their plays.

One of the earliest Indian dramatists to show interest in producing drama for the stage was Asif Currimbhoy, hailed by many as "India's first authentic voice in theatre."[6] His plays—*The Hungry Ones*, *The Captives*, *An Experiment with Truth* etc. reveal a social purpose, a philosophical basis and dexterous stage-craft. Currimbhoy is fully alive to the basics of theatre and maintains that "good theatre does not depend upon language or geography; rather it depends upon inherent situations, and of course, conflict."[7] M.K. Naik, equally conscious of the prerequisites of good theatre visualizes the plight of still born playwrights who lack viable dramatic action.[8]

Some notable contemporaries of Currimbhoy known for their contribution to Indian English drama are Nissim Ezekiel with a volume of three plays to his credit, Gurcharan Das, who based his *Larin Sahib*, a play in three acts, "on events in the Punjab in 1946-47 . . . reconstructed from documents and letters exchanged by the principal characters"[9] and Girish Karnad, who originally wrote in Kannada and then translated his plays into English himself. Shyam Asnani, critically evaluating the works of these playwrights, draws attention to the prevailing misconceptions about the nature of drama.[10] Drama, he says, is not just good literature, it has to be effective as theatre. To endorse his belief he quotes J.K. Styan's assertion that drama is a dramatic construct "realized" in theatre, where the word in the play-text becomes "fleshed out"[11] as it were. A play is a living experience and needs a real theatre and a live audience. Recent attempts at experimentation in theatre-oriented plays are commendable and include works like Pratap Sharma's *A Touch of Brightness*, Shiv K. Kumar's *The Last Wedding Anniversary* and Balwant Gargi's *The Knife*.

Contemporary Indian drama in English translation has made striking innovations and successful experiments in terms of thematic concerns as well as technical virtuosities. It has been increasingly resorting to history, legend, myth and folklore drawing sustenance from their springs of vitality. Mohan Rakesh, Badal Sircar, Vijay Tendulkar and Girish Karnad are vibrant representatives of the Indian drama of the present times in Hindi,

Bengali, Marathi and Kannada respectively. They do, however, also represent Indian drama at the national level for they dramatize universal aspects of modern human life in India.

While Mohan Rakesh presents the total absence of communication between one man and another in contemporary life, Badal Sircar depicts the existential attitude of modern man in the present times. Tendulkar focuses on middle-class life in India and shows the isolated individual's confrontation with adverse circumstances and hostile surroundings. He strongly believes that ideas are firmly entrenched in our psyche at an early age and "our attitudes have a lot to do with what we internalize in our early formative years."[12] Girish Karnad, the Kannada playwright, shows the absurdity of modern life and its passions and conflicts with the help of various myths and legends, his objective being re-interpreting of the past from the vantage-point of the present.

Often compared to luminaries like Henrik Ibsen and Tennessee Williams in his practice of stagecraft, Mahesh Dattani, the thirty-eight year old playwright from Bangalore, along with Manjula Padmanabhan, has given a fresh lease of life to Indian drama in English. Whereas Padmanabhan presents in her plays (for example, in *Harvest*) a dehumanized and unpalatable world. Dattani's works are less grim and forbidding though generally about the unwelcome and unpleasant things of life. What is most notable about Dattani's dramatic art is that the stage for him is no plain expanse of space but a complex multidimensional area in which vital incidents placed in time may be viewed and reassessed, an area in which atmospheric details related to humidity and air-temperature, insignificant though they may seem, are not overlooked. The arena of performance for him is a space in which the written text of a play assumes the form of an enactment and the use of masks represents a deep ritualistic meaning.

Dattani confidently challenges the traditional denotations and connotations of the words "India" and "Indians." He places on them constructs that are far removed from the ones prevalent in modern theatre but are meaningfully related to social, cultural, sexual and religious issues that hold centrestage in life in the present times.

Dattani's theatre group, Playpen, was formed in 1984 and he has directed several of their plays ranging from classical Greek to contemporary works. It was in 1986 that he wrote his first full-length play, *Where There's a Will*, and since then, there has been no looking back. In 1998, he set up his own theatre studio for the grooming of new entrants in acting, directing and stage writing. In the same year he won the Sahitya Akademi award for his anthology of plays, *Final Solutions and Other Plays*, published by East-West Books, Chennai, thus attaining the honour of being the first English language playwright to win the award.

Mahesh Dattani has an array of themes to offer in his plays and the issues he chooses to project are the most topical but also the most controversial ones. *Seven Steps around the Fire* is the heart-rending story of a "hijra" Kamala, who happens to fall in love with the son of an affluent minister named Subbu. When the fact of her being a "hijra" is revealed to people, she is mercilessly murdered. Her deprivation in terms of essential femininity instead of arousing sympathy and a feeling of compassion is looked down upon; she is discriminated against and ultimately murdered. A sense of horror and injustice prevails for it is not by choice but by sheer misfortune that she is what she is.

On a Muggy Night in Mumbai is a tragi-comedy that deals with the travails of the gay community. The play is like a charter of demands for homosexuals whose activities are absolutely taboo in the Indian society. Their sexual proclivities are still strongly forbidden by social custom and are greatly offensive to the prevailing moral and social code. Kiran in the play innocently remarks, "I really wish they would allow gay people to marry." Dattani, here, clearly pleads for social sanction to homosexuals.

Do the Needful is another of Dattani's plays that deals with the problem of homosexuality but what makes it different is that there is grafted onto it a love interest which cannot culminate in marriage because of communal consciousness in the Indian society. The play is a fabric of complex relationships, which expose the fact that the institution of marriage today has lost its sanctity and is nothing but a compromise to promote personal ends. Lata and Alpesh pursue their extra-marital love liaisons even after they have tied the knot, marriage being only an expedient mode of coexistence.

Bravely Fought the Queen deals with women from affluent homes fighting against patriarchal dominance as it prevails in India. The title of the play is derived from a poem in Hindi about the indomitable Rani of Jhansi. Dolly Trivedi, the chief protagonist, has to brave the onslaughts from her violent and unfaithful husband and her tyrannical mother-in-law, who, even in her paralytic, diseased state, holds on to the reins of domestic governance. The technical achievement of Dattani in this play deserves special mention for his realization of the stage as a multi-level space in which time is perceived in its simultaneity and is projected as stratified and tiered.

Tara is predominantly a play about gender discrimination and about the Indian parents' preference for a male child over a female one. It is the story of a pair of twins, a boy, Chandan, and a girl, Tara, who love each other immensely but are separated from each other by design. Tara, persistently maltreated by her mother, eventually dies. Through her death, Dattani demonstrates the unfortunate consequences of differentiation between children on grounds of gender.

Dance Like a Man is a play set in Chennai where dance is an integral part of life and a favourite mode of aesthetic expression. Ratna wants her daughter Lata to achieve distinction as a danseuse as she herself had been thwarted in her desire to make her mark as a dance artist because of the repressive patriarchal dominance exercised by her father-in-law, Amritlal, who expected all the members of his family to prostrate themselves before him. Rebellion surfaces in the family the very moment Amritlal breathes his last.

Where There's a Will is another play in which Dattani's recurrent motif of patriarchal paramountcy appears. A woman is generally looked upon as a commodity; her prime functions in marriage are to dance attendance upon her husband and to be an exciting partner in bed. This undemocratic nature of man is what repulses a woman, be it daughter, wife, daughter-in-law or mistress. The plot of the play revolves around the tyrannical patriarch, Hasmukh Mehta, who is a terror for the members of his family when alive as well as when dead. Even after his death there is no relief for them for he hovers oppressively around them as a ghost, persecuting them as when alive. The humour in the play, however, is a major redeeming factor and has its source largely in the interjections and asides of Hasmukh as a ghost. Also, Dattani's depiction of a visible/invisible and audible/inaudible ghost extends the scope of naturalistic drama.

Dattani's *Final Solutions*, first staged in Bangalore in 1993, focuses on the problem of communal disharmony between the Hindus and Muslims in India, especially during the period of the post-Partition riots. The analysis of the cause of friction between the two communities offered by Dattani carries conviction as it is endorsed by a study of human psychology offering valid explanations of the proclivities and susceptibilities of individuals under circumstantial pressure.

The psychosis that prevails among the Hindus as well as the Muslims in India after the event of the partition of the country causes a chain of neurotic reactions to even the most inconsequential of happenings. Dattani's purpose in depicting the post-Partition communal violence in India at the very outset is not to convey to us events as they actually took place but to impress upon us the consciousness that a more primitive logic now prevails. The realization that there is a total absence of restraint in the perpetration of tragic violence leads us to the painful experience of confronting an advancing foe all set to demolish the human laws of love and mercy. Dattani, however, does not charge his descriptions of the incidents of brutality and monstrosity with feelings; rather, he offers journalistic reports of the events. He bypasses the emotional aspects of the historical situation because it is not to his purpose. He subordinates the specific events of history to an analysis of the situation as it prevails. His focus is on a "failure of understanding"[13] between man and man.

The stance adopted by the various characters in *Final Solutions* is purposefully structured. The experiences of each individual as depicted in the play lead to the discovery of meaning in his or her life. The play opens with Daksha reading lines from her diary. The setting suggests that the period is late 1940s. Daksha is the grandmother of the central character of the play, Ramnik Gandhi. She shuttles between her two identities, namely, that of a girl of fifteen and that of a mature lady who has witnessed forty years of freedom. The Chorus chanting at the back sometimes assume Hindu masks and sometimes Muslim ones. The words rendered by the Chorus are clear indicators of the communal disharmony and its painful consequences that are soon to be experienced by the characters in the play. The masks have a leavening effect on the minds of the characters who wear them. The effective use of the Chorus in the play is a dynamic technique used by the playwright. In the stage directions the dramatist gives clear hints at the nature of the Chorus:

> There are five Hindu masks and five Muslim masks. The mob/chorus become the chorus when they "wear" either the Hindu or the Muslim masks but when referred to individually, they remain Chorus 1, Chorus 2, etc. The players of the Mob/Chorus do not belong to any religion and ideally should wear black.[14]

Ramnik Gandhi saves the two Muslim boys, Bobby and Javed while the Chorus all the while curses the boys and exhorts the people to kill them. It calls Ramnik a "traitor" for protecting the boys. In Act III, the accusations and counter-accusations that are exchanged between Ramnik and Javed intensify the feelings of hatred that exist between them though, later, Javed himself admits that he has been carried away and does not know what he is doing. Soon, however, he is disillusioned. Smita, an essentially secular character, tells her mother not to impose on her anymore religious prejudices. She boldly tells her mother, "You have to admit you are wrong."

Life can be lived peacefully only if anger is expunged from our range of emotions but a state of total exclusion of this feeling from our mental make-up is not really possible. Under such conditions one wonders whether there can ever be any final solutions to the problem of communal violence and hatred. Dattani resolves the play with an inconclusive end and leaves the viewers delving deep in search for an answer to the problem posed. In this context, Javed very pertinently asks "Don't we all have anger and frustration?" (205) It is precisely this frustration resulting in anger that is the undoing of all. The open-ended finale leaves us musing as to what solution there can be to the mutual hatred and intolerance that prevails between the Hindus and Muslims in India. A Hindu has always inherited a preconceived notion of what a Muslim is like. As Vijay Tendulkar in his essay "Muslims and I" points out, "A Muslim was someone you stayed away from." (63)

In the context of the play *Final Solutions* the fears and anxieties of the two communities are largely an aftermath of the Partition but in conservative Hindu homes there has always been a tacit dislike for and disapproval of everything associated with Muslims to the extent that everything touched by the latter is considered to be contaminated. Muslims, too, are conscious of the antipodal position they assume in a Hindu community and are equally averse to the Hindus. This mutual aversion of the two communities for each other in India is not overplayed but is depicted with a rare fidelity which spells absolute conviction. Dattani himself, in his Preface to his anthology of dramatic works, *Collected Plays*, proclaims, "I am certain that my plays are a true reflection of my time, place and socio-economic background." (xv) He wonders what the future of his art in the new millennium will be "in a country that has a myriad challenges to face politically, socially, artistically and culturally." (162)

The play *Final Solutions* adheres sincerely to this economy of words advocated by Rakesh and the theme of communal disharmony is demonstrated largely through action and "dramatic" individual attitudes on the stage itself. Alyque Padamsee, in his introductory lines to the play—"A Note on the Play"—underscores the dramatist's externalization of the "communal hatred and paranoia "lurking inside ourselves" (161) in terms of the mob which is a symbol of this hatred.

Alyque Padamsee talks of moving the play "from printed word to living and breathing characters." (162) Examining *Final Solutions* from the psycho-analytical point of view, Padamsee, who has directed this play of Dattani, defines it as "a play about transferred resentments," (161) about looking for a pretext to unload oneself, to give vent to one's wrath by hitting out at those who cannot retaliate and retort. The play, he feels, deals with the "simmering undercurrents" (161) in a family where Ramnik, the father, voices his resentment at his own father's stealthy and unjust deeds by shouting at his mother, Hardika. Smita, the daughter, hits out at her mother, Aruna, as an outlet to the pent-up emotion within her at her infructuous love for Babban, her friend's fiancé. Hardika, in turn, comes to hate her best friend, Zarine, and her community, the hatred being a mode of spouting her indignation at being subjected to the small-mindedness of her in-laws. Of all the characters in the play, Aruna alone seems confident and well-adjusted only to be charged with nursing religious prejudices that leave the two communities—Hindus and Muslims—in a state of stasis, "ever-locked in combat." (161)

Dattani, in his artistic credo as expressed in his preface to *Collected Plays*, clearly states, "I write for my plays to be performed" (xi) leaving no doubt about the fact that he wants his plays to be a living experience, a communication realized on the stage, a message which is transferred from the page to the stage so that there is a minimal dependence on what Mohan Rakesh calls the "dramatic word."[15]

Dattani's plays, then, have purely performance-oriented scripts that elicit from the audience an emotional as well as a strongly intellectual response. His plays are a commitment to what Iyengar calls the "manifestoes of the new realism"[16] and conform closely to the requirements of a play that communicates, for, as M.K. Naik observes, "a play, in order to communicate fully and become a living dramatic experience, needs a real theatre and a live audience."[17] Dattani has created a vibrant, new theatrical form which is a marked development on the hitherto stagnant Indian drama in English.

NOTES

1. G.N. Devy, "Indian English Literature and Commonwealth Literature," *In Another Tongue* (1993; Madras: Macmillan, 1995), p. 31.
2. *Ibid.*, p. 3.
3. Qtd. *Flowering of Indian Drama*, ed. K. Venkata Reddy and R.K. Dhawan (New Delhi: Prestige, 2004), p. 7.
4. K.R.S. Iyenger, *Drama in Modern India* (Bombay: The P.E.N. All India Centre, 1961), p. 1.
5. Prema Nandakumar, "Indians Writing in English: Three Cheers," *Indian Literature*, Vol. XIII, No. 4 (December, 1970), p. 36.
6. Faubion Bowers, "Introduction," *Asif Currimbhoy's Plays* (New Delhi: Oxford and IBH, n.d.) p. xii.
7. Asif Currimbhoy, "A Personal View of Indo-English Drama," *Indian Drama*, ed. H.H. Anniah Gowda (Mysore: Prasaranpa, 1976), p. 43.
8. M.K. Naik, *Dimensions of Indian English Literature* (New Delhi: Sterling, 1984), p. 157.
9. Gurcharan Das, *Larin Sahib* (Delhi: OUP, 1970), 'Afterword,' p. 87.
10. Shyam Asnani, "Indian English Drama," *Spectrum History of Indian Literature in English*, ed. Ram Sewak Singh and Charu Sheel Singh (New Delhi: Atlantic, 1997), p. 107.
11. J.L. Styan, *The Elements of Drama* (London: Cambridge University Press, 1960), p. 134.
12. Shoma Choudhury and Gita Ranjan, ed., *Vijay Tendulkar* (New Delhi: Katha, 2001), p. 65.
13. B. Rajan, *The Dark Dancer* (New Delhi: Arnold Heinemann, 1976), p. 262. Compare the situation in *Final Solutions* with a similar situation in Balchandra Rajan's novel, *The Dark Dancer*.
14. Mahesh Dattani, *Collected Plays* (New Delhi: Penguin, 2000), p. 165.
15. *The Dramatic World*, a Nehru Memorial Fellowship Project. Mohan Rakesh's notes and letters concerning this project were posthumously published in *Enact*, Vol. 7, 1973.
16. K.R.S. Iyengar, *Indian Writing in English* (Bombay; Asia, 1977), p. 195.
17. M.K. Naik, "The Achievement of Indian Drama in English" *Dimensions of Indian English Literature* (New Delhi: Sterling, 1984), p. 151.

The Dramatic Art of Mahesh Dattani

VANDANA DATTA
R.N. College, Hajipur

Mahesh Dattani is the first Indian playwright writing in English to be awarded the Sahitya Akademi award. The award citation says that Dattani's work "probes tangled attitudes in contemporary India towards communal differences, consumerism and gender . . . a brilliant contribution to Indian drama in English." The producers of Dattani's plays praise him highly because his plays are great in performance and also for his treatment of contemporary themes. The purpose of this paper is to study his art and his plays by putting them in the proper perspective. As it is, India has had a rich tradition in drama. His contribution has to be placed against this tradition in order to assess its value. It is also to be borne in mind that judging a contemporary is not a simple job. The detachment that is required in judging someone comes from distance in time. Only then can things be seen in a proper perspective. Moreover, there are also chances of the artist outgrowing himself. However, while no final judgements can be passed, the trends can always be gauged and an assessment made.

To begin with, the word 'drama' comes from the Greek word *dran*—to do. That is to say, drama is a performing art, a living art in a way that no other genre of literature is. It is an art that involves the playwright, the actors and the audience in a single creative effort. And it is in this context that the Indian English drama cuts a sorry figure. Cut off from the masses that are so vital for its development as a living theatre it has not grown the way Indian English fiction has. This appears a bit ironical considering the rich tradition of drama that India has had. But a cursory glance through the history of drama in India will explain things. Though many of the early dramas have not survived, it is clear that Sanskrit drama developed fairly rapidly in the centuries immediately preceding the Christian era. By 500 B.C. there already existed the *Natyashastra*, a detailed treatise that deals with all aspects of the diverse arts that are embodied in the classical Indian concept of the drama, including dance, music, poetics and general aesthetics. Here Bharata describes drama as mimicry of the actions and conduct of the people (*owasthanukrilirnaalyam*). It follows that it should be rich in various emotions, depicting different situations, relating to men good, bad and indifferent, and gives courage, amusement, happiness and advice to all of them. Whether its origin was religious or secular remains to be decided. But this highly stylized form of drama called *natyadharmi* flourished till about the 10th century A.D. There also existed another form of drama, the realistic or popular drama called *lokdharmi*. This popular theatre which included folk and devotional genres and puppetry and dance dramas continued to exist even when the performance of classical Sanskrit drama ceased. A number of factors were responsible for this. First of all, with the foreign invasions beginning eleventh century A.D. the Hindu kings were replaced by Islamic rulers who forbade theatre. So far Sanskrit drama had thrived on royal patronage. Moreover, Sanskrit gradually ceased to be a language of the masses. Only the elite spoke the language so that Sanskrit drama had only a limited aristocratic audience. The folk theatre and the *natak* companies continued to depend upon the patronage of local kings, ministers, *zamindars* and temples. Gradually they switched over to the local languages and dialects. The subject of the plays invariably being tales from the mythologies, the actors did not require going through rigorous rehearsals. The audience too used to be an active participant in the drama and much of the enjoyment depended on the unpredictability of it all—on how the actor could improvise in the new situation created by the comments of the audience, within the limits of the given narrative.

If Sanskrit drama declined because Sanskrit no longer remained the language of the masses, Indian English drama found it difficult in taking root for the same reason. For lack of audience participation, actual performance in a live theatre was a difficult proposition and Indian English drama grew sporadically as closet drama. Nevertheless, right from the early nineteenth century, plays have been written in English and not without merit. In the pre-independence era Sri Aurobindo, Rabindranath Tagore, T.P. Kailasam, A.S.P. Ayyar, Harindranath Chattopadhyaya and Bharati Sarabhai are names to be reckoned with. But it remains a fact that most of these playwrights could not conceive of a stage to place their plays. Tagore, however, got his plays staged privately at Shantiniketan. Things have improved since independence. Post-independence drama has also benefited by the growing interest abroad in Indian English literature and a number of plays by dramatists like Asif Currimbhoy, Pratap Sharma and Gurcharan Das were successfully staged in Europe and the United States of America. However, these stray performances abroad did not lead to the establishment of a regular school of Indian English drama at home. Even today English dramas are staged only in the metropolitan cities. This is mainly because theatre in the Indian regional languages monopolizes the attention of the masses. And also because the Indian English drama is yet to plant itself in the Indian ethos. There is now an awareness that the traditional forms need to be utilized to revitalize the Indian English theatre.

This new phase of Indian theatrical development happily coincides with the personal development of Girish Karnad as a dramatist. He is one of the first moderns to have experimented with the fusion of the traditional and the modern dramatic forms and content. It is therefore essential to see what Karnad feels and says about his predicament, which applies to that of the Indian English drama as well:

> To my generation, a hundred crowded years of urban theatre seemed to have left almost nothing to hang on to, to take off from. And where was one to begin again? Perhaps by looking at our audience again, by trying to understand what experience this audience expected to receive from theatre? This at least partly meant looking again at the traditional forms that had been sidelined by

> the Parsi theatre. The attempt . . . was not to find and reuse forms that had worked successfully in some other cultural context. The hope, rather, was to discover whether there was a structure of expectations—and conventions—about entertainment underlying these forms from which one could learn. . . . The most obvious starting point should have been the Sanskrit theatre. . . . Along with this court theatre there had existed other, more popular forms—more flexible, varying in their emphasis on formal purity.[1]

While the Sanskrit plays were written as independent works of art, the popular forms do not have a historical record of their growth. But in India, as Girish Karnad rightly points out, "the past is never totally lost; it coexists with the present as a parallel flow. A rich variety of theatre form still exists, with a continuous history stretching over centuries."[2]

These traditional forms offer the urban playwright a lot of technical freedom with the help of music, mime and exotic imagery. And for all the modernization and westernization of the urban life it has never really been cut off from the folk traditions—the past is never totally lost, that is. Ramanujan unambiguously states: "Even in a large modern city like Madras, Bombay or Calcutta, even in western-style nuclear families with their well-planned 2.2 children, folklore . . . is only a suburb away, a cousin or a grandmother away."[3]

The purpose of using folk traditions is not just to define the Indianness of the Indian English theatre but also to achieve a rare insight into the contemporary reality with the help of traditional symbols and images. In *Hayavadana*, Karnad puts the non-naturalistic techniques of masks, chorus, the mixing of human and non-human worlds offered by our traditional theatre to good use. The mask helps him in emphasizing the essential moral nature of the characters. In *Tughlaq*, Karnad challenges the spatial divisions of the Parsi theatre—the stage was divided into shallow and deep, shallow scenes were played in the foreground with a curtain for the backdrop. This spatial division maintained the gulf between the rulers and the ruled, a division that Karnad refused to adhere to in *Tughlaq*. This violation of the spatial hierarchy was a direct result of the intermingling of form and content—the anarchy at the climax of the play couldn't be presented any better than by allowing the 'shallow' to bulge into the 'deep.' It was also a reflection of the changing times—the narrowing of the great divide between the rulers and the ruled, the haves and the have-nots. A parallel trend can be noted in the west too. Earlier the stage conventions required that the plays be about the Upper Orders. If members of the Lower Order appeared, they did so as minor characters, as retainers, prostitutes or more frequently just as 'comics.' In Indian drama such characters were not even allowed to use the entire stage, they were confined to the 'shallow' portion. But after 1930, both in India and in the west, the burgeoning of the democratic spirit made it necessary to seek new means about expressing new ideas about the new people now seen on the stage in central roles. Hence the old stage conventions had to go.

This leads us to an interesting study of stagecraft in Indian theatre thereby highlighting the importance of the innovations introduced by Mahesh Dattani. The earliest Indian stage was a simple platform erected for the purpose in a palace or a temple courtyard with a painted curtain to serve as the backdrop. The playwright did not provide any stage directions leaving everything to the imagination of the director. Much later the Parsi theatre had its own stage-divisions, as we have seen, of 'shallow' and 'deep.' Another school of drama—the realistic theatre—had arisen in the 1930s. It brought social problems to the fore but followed the European stage-setting so that there is just a three-walled living room on the stage where the entire play happens. This is unrealistic because in an Indian home the living room is the face put forward for the strangers. The real issues are discussed and resolved in the inner chambers, in the kitchen and in the backyard where all and sundry are not allowed. In *Naga-Mandala*, Act One, the stage setting is described as follows:

> The locked front door of a house with a yard in front of the house, and on the right, an enormous ant-hill. The interior of the house—the kitchen, the bathroom as well as Rani's room—is clearly seen.[4]

This is a complicated stage-setting, indeed. The exterior, as well as the interior, the kitchen, the bathroom and also the bedroom are clearly visible. Karnad believes that if one has to go to the heart of the issues one has to go inside the house where the real action takes place, to the kitchen where Rani prepares the paste and pours it in the food, in the bedroom where the Naga comes to meet his beloved and in the bathroom where he enters and exits through the drain in the form of a snake. Having just a living room on the stage would have belied the very spirit of the story.

The stage-settings of Mahesh Dattani are even more complex. There are multi-level sets so that the whole interior of the house is visible to the audience. He reaches new heights in *On a Muggy Night in Mumbai* by creating mental spaces—dark expansive areas where the characters are left to their innermost thoughts. It is interesting to note what John McRae, director at the Abelians theatre, Bari, Italy, has to say about him: "Mahesh Dattani is always adventurous in his ways of using the theatrical space at his disposal: multiple levels, breaking the bounds of the proscenium, wondrously inventive use of lighting to give height, breadth and depth"[5]

The stage is the interior of Kamlesh's flat divided into three acting spaces: the living room, beautifully done up in the ethnic fashion; the bedroom hidden behind a gauze wall acquiring some amount of mystery and secrecy; and a completely non-realistic set comprising three levels, black and expansive, 'characters in this area are immediately suspended in a 'shoonya' where they are forced to confront their innermost thoughts. (49) ''The backdrop to all these three areas is the Mumbai skyline which shows through the window of the living room. The partial view of the 'Queen's Necklace' suggests that the flat is located in the upmarket area of Marine Drive. This skyline is something more than just a backdrop. It is the outside world impinging upon the people in the flat—the wedding going on in the compound below is a nagging presence suggestive of the society that expects the individuals to behave in accordance with its well defined code. The kids who find the photo, the people who pester Bunny for his autographs are part of the same society. The way society is shown pressing in becomes all the more significant because of the theme of the play: gay love, partnership, trust and betrayal. Then, the mental spaces are something like Yeats's drama of the mind. The conflict is psychological. The scene between Ed and Kamlesh on the second level of the mental space is designed to evoke answers from the spectator's consciousness. The spectators are also part of the same society, both Ed and Kamlesh realize, that does not consider their relationship beautiful.

Dattani is even more innovative in the way he uses the multilevel sets for flashbacks in *Final Solutions*. Here the stage setting is even more complicated because both exterior and interior are presented on the stage. There is a crescent-shaped ramp, with the ends sloping to the stage level, where most of the action of the Mob/Chorus takes place. Within the confines of the ramp stands a structure suggesting the house of the Gandhis—the living room is on the same level. On an elevation, the kitchen and the puja room have been done in detail. There is another room on another level with a desk and an oil lamp converted to an electric one—suggesting the period of 1940s. This belongs to Daksha, who is in fact the grandmother Hardika, sometimes seen as a girl of fifteen. The stage direction says that 'Hardika should be positioned and lit in such a way that the entire action of the play is seen through her eyes.' The vantage point is Hardika's viewpoint and the need to show her past how and why she has developed a feeling of hatred for the Muslim community brings in the young Daksha, who is in fact Hardika herself. In several scenes Hardika, the grandmother and Daksha, the young bride, are on the same level at the same time, although they are the same person. This ploy effectively shows how the past moulds the present and also how the present reinterprets the past.

Bravely Fought the Queen is a play in which much of the action takes place in the living room of Dolly and Jiten Trivedi, in a posh suburb of Bangalore. This is a play about acting, about hypocrisy. Hence the living room where the so-called moderns of today live an unreal life perhaps just to impress the unknowing guest. It recalls once again what Karnad had said that the living room is the face—the made-up face put forward to strangers. Reality is to be found in the inner chambers—in the kitchen which is a witness to imagined as well as real scandals and upstage in Baa's bedroom: Baa herself is a living embodiment of past carrying her own burden of guilt.

Tara again has a multi-level set. But the only realistic level is the bedsitter of the older Chandan—Dan—in a suburb of London. It is he who is writing the story of Tara from his memory. The Patel's house on the lowest level occupies a major portion of the stage. But it is not real. It is seen only in memory and is therefore meant to be kept as stark as possible. So much of thought has gone into the stage-settings, every small detail is defined. Dattani takes pains to make his stage look as close to the real thing as possible. There is something Shavian about his detailed stage directions and also about his choice of themes. His attempt is to place the India of today in the fore. The themes are picked up from contemporary issues but are invested with universality so that in the ultimate analysis his plays qualify as genuine human dramas. Some of his favourite themes are: sexuality, communal tension, society versus, individual, gender issues, consumerism, etc. For all his similarity with Shaw so far as choosing contemporary issues as themes for his plays, his method of treatment is entirely different. In Shaw there is a preference for ideas over incident the object of which was to make people think and build public opinion on a given issue. The focus is clearly on the verbal, underlined by the fact that Shaw subtitled *Major Barbara* (1905) as 'A Discussion' and *Misalliance* (1910) as 'A Debate in One Sitting.' Some other plays are described as 'Sermon' in the original subtitle. Shaw saw the stage as a pulpit and himself as a prose preacher:

> My plays do not consist of occasional remarks to illustrate pictures, but of verbal fencing matches between protagonists and antagonists, whose thrusts and ripostes, parries and passados, follow one another much more closely than thunder follows lightning. The first rule for their producers is that there must never be a moment of silence from the rise of the curtain to its fall.[6]

No wonder then that in terms of performance Shaw's plays are anti-naturalistic. Dattani too takes up an issue and is out to prove a point but he does not allow the play to be reduced to the level of a discussion. Even in *On a Muggy Night in Mumbai*, which of all of Dattani's plays comes closest to a discussion, there is plenty of dramatization. It is true that all through the three acts there is no change of scene except for Kamlesh, Kiran and Ed moving up to the empty space for sometime during the second act. Almost the whole of the play is a single scene—Kamlesh has invited his friends to his flat. They—Sharad, Deepali, Ranjit, and Bunny—come and sit through the whole play talking. But it is during their conversation that the knots of the complex relationships open up. Kamlesh and Prakash were lovers once and Kamlesh found it difficult to cope with his separation from Prakash. Sharad helped him get over the trauma. The two were carrying on happily until Kamlesh jilted Sharad. On this particular evening Kamlesh has invited all his friends over to his place to make them promise that they would never mention his affair with Prakash to anyone, to his sister Kiran in particular who has undergone the trauma of a divorce and is now about to marry Ed. Both the relationships of Kamlesh and Prakash and that of Kiran and Ed are delicately poised until the revelation at the climax of the first act that Prakash and Ed are the same person. Though there seems to be little movement in this play, the characters sit together and talk and through their talk tension builds up to a climax of revelations and self-discoveries. Each act has its own build-up, its own dramatic confrontation and its own climax and revelation. And in this dramatic confrontation it is not just the characters who are involved but also the audience. As the play draws towards the end the true face of the characters are revealed and the audience is made to go through catharsis of emotions. In the end Ed emerges as the most pathetic character, Kamlesh too loses the sympathy of the audience. But what the dramatist really wants to show is that it is not just the fault of the characters. It is the society that encourages such hypocrisy by not allowing the Individual to be what it wants to be. Society imposes its own norms one must conform to. Not following them is a sign of perversity. Homosexual relationship is not permitted—hence the entire hide and seek. Hence Kamlesh suffers, Bunny leads a double life—denies his own nature when he says he is 'happily married'; Ranjit has chosen the easy way out by leaving India for Europe where he can be more himself; and Ed turns out to be the biggest victim of his own double game. An extract from the play explains the situation clearly:

Kiran: I really wish they would allow gay people to marry.
Ranjit: Oh, they do. Only not to the same sex.

Dattani is not interested in revealing where his sympathies lie but society versus individual is a theme to which he goes back again in *Dance Like a Man*. Here it is the family—family as the microcosm of society—that lays down its unwritten rules. Jairaj follows his heart's desire and becomes a dancer but has enraged his father in the process. Amritlal Parekh is disappointed because his son's ideas of happiness do not fit in with his. He says: "I have always allowed you to do what you have wanted to do. But there comes a time when you have to do what is expected of you. Why must you dance?" (415) Understandably enough, it is not easy for Jairaj to dance to a different tune and there are times when he wonders whether it has been worth all the sacrifices. All his life he has tried to achieve perfection but has always made mistakes. It is only after their death that he and Ratna, free from the demands of family and society, are able to "dance perfectly. In unison. Not missing a step or a beat." (447) To reach this stage, they have paid a great price—Jairaj has compromised on his manliness and Ratna on her motherhood. One of Jairaj's deepest regrets till the end is that he has not been able to dance like a man. Ratna has been a successful dancer but she has had to pay the price with the life of her son, Shankar and for the rest of her life the albatross hangs from her neck. So strong is the feeling of this guilt that the mere mention of her child's name puts her off.

Such is life. Once a wrong is done it has to be borne all along. There is Baa, in *Bravely Fought the Queen,* a living embodiment of the past carrying her own burden of guilt. Her granddaughter Daksha was born a spastic because of her. She had provoked her son Jiten to beat his wife Dolly because her mother was her father's mistress. The guilt hangs heavy on Baa once she realizes her fault. But the damage is done. She tries to make up for it by giving away her house to Daksha and making Praful the trustee. Nothing, however, can alter the fact that Daksha is not a normal child. The tragedy is writ large in the scene where Dolly reveals that her child was seriously disabled at birth by Jiten's violence. She begins to dance as Daksha would dance—a disjointed movement that a spastic would make. There is no atonement for this crime: the guilt must live on. Michael Walling, the producer of this play in London, gives the greatest tribute to the playwright when he says: "'Isn't that the way she dances?' It seems an innocuous line on the page. But this writing is writing beyond words: this is theatre."[7]

This theme of carrying guilt comes up again with some variation in *Final Solutions.* Ramnik Gandhi—there's lots in a name, it's not for nothing that Ramnik has been given the surname Gandhi—carries the guilt of the wrongs committed by his father and grandfather. They had got Zarine's shop—Zarine was a friend of Hardika—burnt up in the name of communal hatred and later bought it at half its value. Hardika does not know the whole truth. She was given to understand that they were asking for a price much higher than what they deserved. Hence the resentment. As a result Hardika spends all her life hating them and their community. She does not appreciate Ramnik's liberal attitude towards the two Muslim boys who have taken shelter in their home during the riots. But Ramnik has been living with this shame all these years. He has nothing against his wife personally but he cannot stand her rigidity in religious matters because it reminds him of his father's sin. To make up for the wrong committed by his father, he offers Javed a job at the shop. He wants to set things right but it does not happen that way. The boys leave and Ramnik and Hardika are left behind to live on with their shame. Much as Ramnik may want, he fails to find a final solution to his problem.

In *Tara* the context is different, the issue in question is different, but the guilt is very much the same—the ramifications are different. The play deals with the cultural constructions of gender that always gives preference to the male over the female. Tara and Chandan are conjoined twins whose physical separation is manipulated by their mother and grandfather to favour the boy over the girl. The twins had three legs between them. The tests showed that the girl provided a major part of the blood supply to the third leg. Chances were that it would survive on the girl. But the mother had a private meeting with the doctor and bribed him to agree to give both the legs to the boy. The whole effort went in vain because the leg very soon became a lump of dead flesh on Chandan and had to be amputated. To think that it would have been part of Tara! The mother, however, becomes a psychological case. Her guilt eats her up from within and she does not live long. It is Chandan who lives with the shame of it all. He escapes to London, changes his name to Dan, and tries to repress the guilt by living in a strange land. Failing to do so, he tries to get over it by writing the story of Tara but ends up writing the story of his own childhood and discovers:

> Locking myself in a bedsitter in a seedy suburb of London, thousands of miles from home hasn't put enough distance between us. . . . Maybe we still are. Like we've always been. Inseparable. The way we started in life. Two lives and one body, in one comfortable womb. Till we were forced out. . . . And separated. (323-25)

Gender discrimination is a theme that Mahesh Dattani returns to again and again. In *Bravely Fought the Queen* and *Where There's a Will* one of the concerns is the complicated modern urban family where the old patriarchal code finds a formidable foe in the new feminist ideas. In the former play, living a suppressed life drives the women to indulge in fantasies. What they miss out in real life they achieve in their dreams. It requires great courage on the part of the writer to take up such subjects that are taboo in India. While feminism has become acceptable, a middle-class housewife having a sex life or even fantasizing about one is certainly not acceptable. Dolly emerges as a strong and beautiful woman who is a rebel not only in fantasies but also in reality. She bravely holds her ground against her husband Jiten even in front of a stranger. She defends her sister and her brother and makes it clear that she can never forgive her husband for causing the abnormality in their daughter. But the fact remains that even today women are expected to be subordinated to the men. *Where There's a Will* shows what can happen when they are pushed to the edge. However, this play has many interesting facets. It is a very entertaining comedy and a strong comment on the moneymindedness of people today—even personal relationships are based on money. Wife, son, daughter-in-law—all are interested only in the huge amount of wealth that garment tycoon Hasmukh Mehta has acquired. The most interesting aspect of this play, however, is the philosophical angle given to it. After his death Hasmukh's ghost stays on in the house observing all that's going on. And now comes the realization that it is not just the members of his family who are to blame. It is as much his fault. All his life he has controlled his family not through love and affection but through his money. Even after his death he tries to rule over them through his will. Kiran, his mistress, who is the trustee of the will for twenty-one years, is right that the only reason he wanted to do this is because his father had ruled over his family. He never really grew out of his father's shadow, never really tried to understand his people and therefore became a victim of his own machinations.

Dattani's plays have deep moral undertones but never really does he take on the stance of the moralist, never raises himself to a pedestal from where he could preach. He treats his characters with understanding and sympathy whether they are good or bad, right or wrong. He never pronounces any rewards or punishments, thereby allowing the natural law of justice to prevail. He seems to be a genuine artist in love with his art. His plays are meant to be performed, not just read as literature—a fact corroborated by Erin Mee, a theatre director: "It is important to note that all of Dattani's plays, including *Tara*, are first workshopped with his company Playpen in Bangalore. Dattani puts the finishing touches on his dialogue only when it is spoken aloud by actors in rehearsal—in other words, Dattani writes plays to be seen and heard, not literature to be read."[8] The sad part is that Indian drama in English is yet to gain a sizeable audience in India. "No wonder Dattani's plays address the middle-class and only the middle class. The reason is not far to seek—it is this class that constitutes his audience. The language barrier prevents the lower classes from coming to the Indian English theatre. But with the spread of education and the circumstances that make learning English a prerequisite for a good career one may just hope that things may not remain the same for long. For tomorrow is another day.

NOTES

1. Girish Karnad, "Introduction," *Three Plays* (New Delhi: Oxford University Press, 1994), p. 11.
2. *Ibid.*, p. 12
3. A.K. Ramanujan, "Introduction," *Folktales from India* (New Delhi: Viking, 1993), p. xiii.
4. Girish Karnad, *Naga-Mandala*, in *Three Plays*, p. 27
5. John McRae, "A Note on the Play," *On a Muggy Night in Mumbai*, in *Collected Plays: Mahesh Duttani* (New Delhi: Penguin India, 2000), p. 45.
6. George Bernard Shaw, qtd. Christopher Innes, *Modern British Drama 1890-1990* (Britain: Cambridge University Press, 1992), p. 21.
7. Michael Walling, "A Note on the Play," *Bravely Fought the Queen*, in *Collected Plays*, p. 230.
8. Erin Mee, "A Note on the Play," *Collected Plays*, p. 320

Dattani's Exercise in Postcolonialism

GAURI SHANKAR JHA
I.G. Govt. College, Tezu

Dattani is 'altogether different' in his approach and presentation. While talking of Dattani, Rehmat Merchant says, "Mahesh Dattani's pathos-with-a-punch approach, picked with a dash of humour, makes him the perfect candidate for chronicling urban angst. His plays are peopled with city slickens wrestling with issues in a manner close to the modern psyche . . . change-the-world brand of range and impulsiveness, threatens to upset some apple carts . . . subtext of complex relationships . . . eager to understand mind contrasted by informed prejudice . . . character growing . . . build in conflict in marriage . . . collapse of certain stereotypes . . . prejudice holder forced to look outside the cosy community circle."[1] Dattani is taken to be a true successor of Girish Karnad and responsible for the revolutionary progression of Indian English drama, as a drama teacher, as a stage director, as an actor, as a Bharatnatyam dancer and as a sociologist explaining various complexities of society. Dattani's contribution is an asset to Indian writing as a whole.

Indian writing comprises plethora of plays, in other words, playwrights dictate the making of Indian writing. The rich and varied Indian dramatic tradition, the 'fifth Veda,' enshrined in *Natyasastra*, expounded by Bharatmuni, is enviable to the other writings of the world literature. Indian English writing, too, has sufficient number of plays, with a history that can never be accepted as steady or consistent. K.R. Srinivasa Iyengar is highly depressed at the dismal sight of the birth and progress of Indian English drama: "Modern Indian dramatic writing in English is neither rich in quantity, nor on the whole of quality. Enterprising Indians have for nearly a century occasionally attempted drama in English but seldom for actual production."[2]

In the same way Dhyaneshwar Nadkarni declares in "Butcher the Indo-Anglians," "Butcher them (the Indo-Anglian playwrights), castrate them and force them to write in their native Hindi or Urdu or whatever languages their fathers and mothers used to speak." However, the postcolonial scenario is completely different, at least with the advent of Karnad and Dattani, the present practitioners like Vera Sharma, Derek Antao, Gieve Patel, Shashi Tharoor, Khushwant Singh, Nissim Ezekiel, Dina Mehta, Uma Parameswaran, Manjula Padmanabhan, T.S. Gill, J.P. Das, S. Vasuki, G. Prasanti, R. Raj Rao, Leo Fredricks, Saros Cowasjee, Suraj Purohit, Bina Bhakta, etc., we find a quantum jump (so to say).

Pre-colonial, colonial and postcolonial experiences in literature cannot be compartmentalised in true sense, they are not divorced from each other, rather a continuous process, recording the vicissitudes of time. Successive waves of colonisation have left its vestiges in the natural psyche and national polity, and the near schizophrenic scenario is a colonial legacy accumulated over centuries, pre-independence political preoccupations centred on idealisation, generalisation, mystification, etc. available in contemporary literature. In fact, commonwealth literature has been rechristened as postcolonial literature and Indian writing in English is a legitimate product of our historical and existential conjectures, a genuine expression of our profound postcolonial civilisational crisis, signifying the disparity between the publicity it attracts and its literary quality and ability to reflect our social and spiritual lives. Like other subaltern theories of literature, postcolonialism stands for those who have been sentenced by history to subjugation, diaspora and displacement, empowering the marginalised by retrieving the voices, space and identities silenced by colonial power. In Indian English writing, postcolonial exits from Raja Rao to Salman Rushdie, among several others, in the plays of Girish Karnad, Vijay Tendulkar, Mahesh Elkunchwar, etc. the complexities of postcolonialism being inherited from the colonial and pre-colonial times. Like Arthur Miller and Arnold Wesker, Asif Currimbhoy is critical of values, materialism, corruption, frivolity, etc. With the reform-oriented movements of the nineteenth century began the major phase of anticolonialism which sought the tradition to be re-examined. In the modernism of the Fifties and Sixties, there was also a pan Indian shift in sensibility, for instance, the Dalit movement, the women's movement, etc. In modernising postcolonial tension and anxieties are visible the colonial education, ruthless urbanisation, inhuman industrialisation, loss of faith, erosion of ethos, challenges to the identity, etc.

Mahesh Dattani emerges as a compelling playwright who rearranges the social fabrication and projects the postcolonial dichotomy operating at different levels. Commenting upon the nature of postcolonial writing, Taher Ben Jallouin, a writer from Morocco, says; "We have two cultures, it is as if we had two mothers and two fathers, perhaps we don't have total control, like writers in the West, but we have two possible inner worlds, I think we are doubly clever; firstly to use the narrative techniques of the West and secondly, to exploit the narrative traditions, of the folklore, the stories from our respective countries, and we have come up a third type of literature which is unlike Western writing, which is essential provincial, egocentric and onward looking. We have created literature which is open to other cultures and situations"[3]

Dattani belongs to the section of writers who established women at the centre of their fictive world and may be called avant grade feminist. Western education has a liberating influence on women, bringing promise of a new life outside the claustrophobic environment of purdah and other conservative measures. The response is so eager and unselfconscious that is ready to welcome the accident with gestures of mutual exchanges. Thematically that did not desist from the portrayal of the Indian background; they offered the gifts of the East in the form of Sanskrit epics and Hindu myths and legends.

Mahesh Dattani is to be estimated on two counts: first his concern for the fair sex and second his visit to the virgin landscapes, that is, of homosexuals, eunuchs, etc. Kiran, the mistress of Hasmukh in *Where There's a Will*, Ratna the wife of Jairaj in *Dance Like a Man*, Tara the protagonist in the play *Tara*, Old

Baa, Dolly and Alka in *Bravely Fought the Queen*, Deepali in *A Muggy Night in Mumbai*, Gowda and Lata in *Do the Needful* and Uma in *Seven Steps around the Fire* are faced with the feminine question of identity and dilemma of feminine sensibility to an extent that it brings forth the colonial perspectives of society. Gayatri Spivak in 'Can the Subaltern Speak?' analyses the question of female subaltern, when she describes women as doubly marginalized subjects in colonial/postcolonial discourses: "Within the effaced itinerary of the subaltern subject the track of sexual difference is doubly effected. . . . It is rather, that, both as object of colonialist historiography and as subject of insurgency, the ideological construction of gender keeps the male dominate, if, in the context of colonial production, the subaltern has no history and cannot speak, the female as female is more deeply in shadow."[4] Spivak quotes female subaltern as "doubly effected," the "otherness" of postcolonial literature. Kiran, the mistress of Hasmukh in *Where There's a Will* and Ratna, the wife of Jairaj in *Dance Like a Man*, both belong to the postcolonial era, the "new" women bold and self-confident. Deepali confirms it in her statement: "Every time I mensurate, I thank God I am a woman. (*A Muggy Night in Mumbai*)[5]

On the other hand, we have Sonal under strict vigilance of her elder-sister Minal (in *Where There's a Will*), Tara (in *Tara*) a victim of sex discrimination, Old Baa, Dolly and Alka victim of different trends (in *Bravely Fought the Queen*): Old Baa deserted by her husband, all alone in her last phase of life, Dolly, victim of a brutal husband, beaten in an advanced stage of pregnancy to give birth to a deformed daughter, and Alka the wife of a homosexual. Minal's over-possessive nature snatches Sonal's liberty and she is almost crippled and handicapped for the rest of her life like Laura of Tennessee Williams' *The Glass Menagerie* and Herbert of W.S. Maugham's *The Kite*.

Old Baa, Dolly, Alka and Tara are victims of patriarchal society. Going by tradition, women's lives have been organised and manipulated by patriarchy in all ages, all cultures and all countries by establishing values, norms, roles, gender perceptions and idealism that prescribe unequal means, methods and routes to achieve the so-called 'wholeness' for women. Motherhood and wifehood are the dual crowns of womanhood. In *Where There's a Will*, Minal complains: "Even at my husband's funeral, she sat beside me and told me when to cry." Adrienne Rich emphasizes the absurdity of the situation: "Though motherhood is the experience of women, the institution of motherhood is under male control and the physical situation of becoming a mother is disciplined by males. This glorious motherhood imposed on women conditions her entire life."[6] Barbara Christian explains, "Ironically, the experience unique to women is interpreted for them through male authorities and structures, through religions, myths, science, politics, economics."[7]

Dattani's women suffer as a traditional commodity as Tara in the play *Tara* and Old Baa, Dolly and Alka in *Bravely Fought the Queen*. On the contrary, we have Kiran and Ratna, emerging as emphatic postcolonial woman. The chasm between the two categories of women presents the rift between colonial consciousness and postcolonial compulsion. It is here that we find the postcolonial dichotomy and perhaps Dattani unconsciously hints at the plight of women, torn between being and becoming. The overall impact of colonial consciousness has made us class conscious, creating situation for women liberation, deepening the feeling of self-centredness and proneness to materialism. The postcolonial writers thematically offered the gifts of the East in the form of Sanskrit epics and Hindu myths and legends, they also did not desist from the portrayal of the Indian background, an indispensable adjunct of their own loved clime. Far from becoming sycophantic instruments of the imperial infiltration of Indian culture and literature, they sought to enrich by contributing to it some of their own Indian and feminine perception of the world. Dattani belongs to the same race. He is like Kafka and Camus, Sartre and Saul Bellow, Elison and Malamud. His central characters are product of colonial consciousness and they are in search of their lost self, their identity like Blanche Dubois of Tennessee Williams or Willy Loman of Arthur Miller. As Karl Marx observes in 1853, the British colonization of India had a double mission: "The annihilation of Old Asian society and the laying of the material foundation of Western society in Asia." They brought to India English liberalism, rule of law, individual rights, land reforms, etc. as their regenerating role. In their destructive role, the British cunningly imposed the Western materialistic values as Indian culture and civilization. Their shrewd attempt was to transform the Indian psyche through a system of education. As Aime Cesaire says: "I am talking of societies drained of their essence, cultures trampled underfoot, institution undermined, lands confiscated, religions smashed, magnificent, artistic creations destroyed, extraordinary possibilities wiped out." (21) There is a sharp contrast to the Indian tradition that is essentially non-acquisitive in its emphasis and values but had to undergo cataclysmic change. The erosion of enduring tradition brought dichotomy in the postcolonial writings.

The second proposition of my paper is Dattani's preference for the virgin field, that of homosexuals, eunuchs, etc. To some extent, in Indian writing, this comes in the realm of taboo. Though he is not the first to visit this unexplored piece of land, his approach is certainly different. *Bravely Fought the Queen* has Alka's husband as homosexual but in *A Muggy Night in Mumbai* homosexuality is the core issue, a team of affluent lesbians and sodomists. All the characters in the play—Kamlesh, Sharad, Ed, Prakash, Bunny, Ranjit and Deepali—fight with their own prejudices and end in meaningless nothingness. The questions that haunt Dattani are: (a) Is homosexuality assertion of individuality? (b) Is it guided by some conviction? (c) Does it lead to some meaningful goal? (d) What is the utility of marriage to such people? (e) Can they think of a better future? (f) Does it affect the life as a whole in a positive way? (g) Should human life be interpreted in terms of sex only? (h) Is it an alternative to established norms? (I) Is it quest for some exclusive identity? I feel, most of the questions remain unanswered. And so is Dattani who proves inconclusive in his drive towards settlement of such controversies. It is neither the question of subaltern nor resistance nor appropriation nor reconstruction—for which postcolonial literature stands—rather it is the failure of postcolonial claims to resolve all complications in a unique way—the widespread dichotomy: a woman compelled to "jump into a bottomless pit." (*Where There's a Will*)

Seven Steps around the Fire, the most popular play, dwells on the theme of eunuchs, their identity, their constitution and their connotation. Uma Rao, the sociology scholar, emerges as the most powerful character of the play, the mouthpiece of the playwright, who fights to establish the identity of an eunuch, Kamala, during her research on the class and gender-related violence and crime, its justice in the nemesis of the play. An eunuch, a beautiful one, invited for marriage, and the final tragic death—all seem to be a misconstruct. But it happens. The mystery behind the death is there in the police-politician-crime nexus which is a postcolonial development. Mr. Sharma, the nasty politician does not understand the importance of marriage which is a sacred institution, accepted throughout the globe. The evidence is destroyed but the consciousness remains. Dattani's deconstruction of his own beauty parlance is a postmodernist approach: "I scratched her face, hoping she will become ugly and Sabbu will forget her. She was beautiful. Very beautiful. That is why Salim's wife put fire to her beautiful skin and burned her to the other world." (41, 15) It seems to reflect the postcolonial trend, that is discourse of subversion and liberation against the politics of hegemony. Dattani appears to be a reformist, with a setting both traditional and modern, unable to find out any alternative/solution. This genderless sub-group also constructs its mark of difference, its femininity by wearing saris. As Champa makes it clear, in different situations they can construct their gender and deploy their difference to their own advantage. The power to occupy different subject positions rests entirely in themselves; they create and deny difference, this makes a moment of rapture in the plays, apparent celebration of contingency and situatedness, in that it is an ambivalent other that discovers or reveals a fixed form of difference. This gesture can be read as a revelation only insofar as we recognise some form of fixed system of representation. It is a difference, or rather a certain set of social, political and ideological conditions in a specific context which affirm the view that this particular kind of ethnicity and another context that problematize the creation of ethnic difference highlights the dichotomy of postcolonial writings. The dichotomy of the play is operative at another level, that is, the difference between the findings of social science and the reluctance of implementing authorities. The weakness of judiciary, that depends on evidence only, is also remarkable. The play speaks of subaltern and thus fulfills the postcolonial condition of writing.

The most remarkable element which Dattani highlights is the absurdity of the situation in which the woman is trapped by birth. In *Bravely Fought the Queen*, he presents the same picture; traditionally bound, organized and manipulated by patriarchy in all ages by established values, norms, roles, and gender perceptions, they are guided by idealism that prescribes unequal means, methods and routes to achieve the so-called 'wholeness' for women, motherhood and wifehood being the dual crowns of womanhood. It is the man who has defined this unequivocal term, as motherhood is disciplined by males and they further justify themselves through religions, myths, science, politics, economics etc.

Homosexuality is another significant subject matter chosen by Dattani. In *Bravely Fought the Queen*, Dattani takes up the problem of homosexuality of a married man which ultimately mars his conjugal life. Old Baa's second-daughter-in law Alka has to suffer the reluctance of her husband who is a big failure in his business, just because he is in the trap of this dangerous sexual disease. The same theme occupies the central slot in the play *A Muggy Night in Mumbai*. Here it seems to be a hobby of the elite class of society. M.K. Naik calls it the record of "Their changing mutual relationship, their revelations, their self discussion and self discoveries, though they are all sailing in the same boat; each has his/her own oar to put in his/her own flag to hoist." We have a female character Deepali, too, who is an aggressive lesbian. All characters—Kamlesh, Sharad, Ed, Bunny, Ranjit and Deepali—seem to be of different constitution but equally defiant of the institution called marriage, ridiculing the wedding music in the final Act. Dattani's *Do the Needful* also culminates in confessions of homosexuality by Alpesh whose hope for a better life is ruined for the same reason. Perhaps Dattani projects homosexuality as mode of sexual perversion which finally drags one down, isolating from the social platform, destroying conjugal relationship, forcing to suffer in solitude. It also points towards the postcolonial design and concept that is responsible for dichotomy evident in its continuous erosion of moral and spiritual values and discipline.

Dattani's apparent affirmation of the self's ability to inhabit a multiplicity of subject positions occurs within what Homi K. Bhabha calls in *Nation in Narration* "the instability of cultural signification" that is articulated as a "dialectic of various temporalities—modern, colonial, postcolonial, native," the boundaries of these temporalities constantly interrupt one another in which the retrieval of the past to construct differences/problematic notion of fixedness and essentialness. This instability of cultural significance does not lead to limitlessness of representation but opens up spaces in which the significance functions on the level of temporality whose inflections are governed by changing cultural and social practices. Kirin Narayan's *Love, Stars and All That* also presents eunuchs, their ambivalent gestures as exposure and affirmation of fixedness and negation of ethnic differences functioning as referential system of representation but in all the cases ethnicity is situational.

Aime Cesaire in *Discourse in Colonialism* seems to be highly factual in his observation of what colonization has destroyed; "the wonderful Indian civilization—and neither Deterding nor Royal Dutch nor standard Oil will ever console me for the Aztecs and the Incas." All this results in dichotomy. Colonization brought materialism and mechanism, in sharp contrast to the Indian value-based tradition. The perception of life underwent a thorough change—the contemplative, centripetal, spiritual and temporal transformed to realistic, centrifugal, material, historical and temporal—leading to erosion of enduring traditional values. That is why Dattani's characters "come alive in their relationship." His cry of dichotomy is apparent in *Do the Needful* where outcasts are agents of change, 'moderns' here are the ones with no alternatives and as Dattani says, "Change doesn't happen overnight, we grow liberal often not because we want to, but have to." It is a keen study of the modern psyche.

Perhaps Dattani's intention is to achieve a harmony (that is missing) through the language of theatre, as he comments in his talk on 11 Feb. 2001 at Ravindra Kalakshetra as part of the Krishi Festival Plays to celebrate the 50th Anniversary of Bengali Theatre in Bangalore.

> Man has created a very complex language called theatre. A language that has the ability to redefine the natural concepts of time, space and movement. A language that goes beyond the verbal, a movement that goes beyond the physical. Through this language of theatre he has been able to see himself for who he is, what he has made of himself and what he aspires to be.[8]

His earnest desire is to have identity of our own and, "to form our cultural identities we need all three: traditions, continuity and change. It is when we accept the need for all three in our theatre that we can truly have a theatre movement that is inextricably linked to the development of cultural, social and individual identities."[9]

NOTES

1. R Merchant on M. Dattani, *India Today*, Feb. 14, 2000.
2. K.R.S. Iyengar, *Indian Writing in English* (New Delhi: Sterling, 1985), p. 226.
3. T.B. Jallotin, Interview with V. Naravani, *The Sunday Times of India*, Jan. 28, 1996.
4. G.C. Spivak, "Can the Subaltern Speak," *The Postcolonial Studies Reader*, ed. Bill Ashcroft, et al.
5. M. Dattani, *Collected Plays* (New Delhi: Penguin India, 2000).
6. A. Rich, *Of Woman Born* (New York: Bantam, 1967), p. 45.
7. B. Christian, *Black Feminist Criticism: Perspectives on Black Women Writer* (New York: Pargamon Press, 1985), p. 2.
8. Mahesh Dattani, "Contemporary Indian Theatre and Its Relevance," *Journal of Indian Writing in English*, Vol. 30, No. 1, Jan. 2002, p. 1.
9. *Ibid*, p. 4.

The Plays of Mahesh Dattani: A Fine Fusion of Feeling and Form

AMAR NATH PRASAD
Jagdam College, Chapra

For the healthy growth of any art, both feeling and form should walk hand in hand. However deep and profound the feeling of an artist be, it fails to arouse poetic response in readers if it is not well formed. Both feeling and form are reciprocal. They are not two separate entities e.g. train and engine or boat and boatman; they are like a tree in which its different parts make an organic whole. A true art is meant for teaching and preaching. Its primary duty is to give delight; its purpose is chiefly aesthetic. History is replete with several instances where only those poets and artists reached the zenith of perfection who maintained a perfect blending of both feeling and form. To me, Mahesh Dattani comes in this category of writers who champion the cause of true art, free from any theory, universal in taste and flavour, appealing to all sections of society, never bound to any caste, class and creed.

Theatre, according to Mahesh Dattani, "is a reflection of what you observe. To do anything more would be to become didactic and then it ceases to be theatre."[1] What Dattani observes can well be seen in almost all his plays where he has tried his best to assimilate both matter and manner. Although each and every play of Dattani raises some prominent issues concerning the various maladies contaminating the healthy tissues of the society, he is never seen didactic and straightforward in his attitude. He knows the art of expressing the views through some powerful images, symbols, stage direction and other means of art. Dattani himself observes that in his plays, "Everything is geared towards rasa."[2] Michael Walling thinks that the plays of

Mahesh Dattani "fuse the physical and special awareness of the Indian theatre with the textual rigour of western models like Ibsen and Tennessee Williams. It is a potent combination, which shocks and disturbs, through its accuracy, and its ability to approach a subject from multiple persepectives. Postcolonial Indian and multi-cultural Britain both have an urgent need for a cultural expression of the contemporary; they require public spaces in which the mingling of eastern and western influences can take place. Through his fusion of forms and influences, Mahesh creates such a space."[3]

His radio play *Seven Steps around the Fire* shows Dattani a master delineator of language and characterization. "Here was a playwright who was not afraid to be powerful without ever being melodramatic."[4] It beautifully deals with the pathetic plight of atmosphere where a minister had the young hijra burned to death. Uma, the daughter of the Vice-Chancellor of Bangalore University and a postgraduate student of sociology, uncovers the truth behind the murder of a hijra. Unlike a sleuth, she uses uncommon means to discover the truth. She boldly goes to the locality of the hijra community and asks them questions. Her attitude to the eunuchs is very friendly and sympathetic. Though her husband Suresh Rao is the chief superintendent of police, he is unable to solve the knots of the mysterious murder of a hijra. Constable Munswamy, who was tasked by Suresh Rao with keeping his wife out of danger, creates a sense of humour and makes the story more enjoyable. Kamala, a beautiful hijra (eunuch), has been secretly married to Subbu, the son of a government minister. The minister got this hijra burned to death and arranged a marriage reception for his son to marry an acceptable girl of his choice. But the table is turned. At the wedding, all the hijras sing and dance and Subbu in a fit of anger, takes out a gun and kills himself.

What matters most in this brief play is the proper use of some words and phrases symbolizing the character and activities of the hijras. Let us see an example.

Interior. The office of the Superintendent of Police

Anarkali: We make our relations with our eyes. With our love. I look at him, he looks at me, and he is my brother. I look at you, you look at me, and we are mother and daughter. Oh, brother, give me a cigarette, na.

Munswamy: Shut up. And don't call me brother.

Anarkali: Just one, na (very sexual) I will do anything for you, brother. Give, na.

Munswamy: Chee! Who would want to . . . (flustered) I—I don't smoke.

Anarkali: If you had a beautiful sister, you will give her a cigarette for a fuck, no

Munswamy: Just because madam is here . . .

Anarkali: · You are not a sister-fucker?

Munswamy: Just talk to madam and then I will see you.

Anarkali I don't want to talk to madam! I want a cigarette!!

Uma: I think there are some here. My husband must be keeping his Gold Flakes here somewhere . . . (opens a drawer) Aha!

Anarkali: (Delighted) Oh!

Uma: Here,

Anarkali: One for the night. One for the morning.

Uma: Keep the whole pack. (11)

This conversion shows how the hijras who are also the members of the society generally speak in a friendly way. But if somebody, like Munswamy, misbehaves, they give a good retort, even go to the extent of speaking rude and vulgar expressions.

In the very beginning of the play we see how hijras are treated like non-living things; they are given the pronoun 'it/its' by characters like Munswamy who has a strong grudge against them. On the other hand, Uma, the protagonist, always behaves sisterly with them and uses the words 'she/her' for them.

Munswamy: You may see the hijra now if you wish, madam.

Uma: Will *she* talk to me?

Munswamy: (Chuckling) *she*! Of course *it* will talk to you. We beat *it* up if *it* does not. (1, my italics)

In another important conversion between Uma and Champa, the readers/ spectators find how being absolutely hated and neglected, the hijras generally develop a sense of frustration and isolation and that they are not the bonafide members of society. Their inner yearnings for being the members of society is seen in the laconic speech of Champa:

Champa: Oh! so you are a social worker. Say that.
Uma: Yes . . . I am a social worker.
Champa: Please excuse me, madam. I didn't know that. . . . You see us also as society, no?

Thus, *Seven Steps around the Fire* expresses the identify crisis of the hijras and their heart-felt longing for being treated as a social being in an indifferent society where people like the government minister seldom feel a qualm of conscience in getting a hijra burnt to death.

In both theme and style, the three-act play *On a Muggy Night in Mumbai* bears the stamp of great craftsmanship. It deals with the gay themes of love, homosexual vulgarity among the youths in a materialistic world, partnership, trust and betrayal. It is "a play about how society creates patterns of behaviour and how easy it is for individuals to fall victim to the expectations society creates."[4] Almost all the characters of this play are types of certain behaviour which reminds us of the Restoration plays and sentimental comedies specially Sheridan's *The Rivals* and *The School for Scandal*. The drama also contains some powerful symbols, images and stage directions which cannot help without arousing aestheticism and rich poetry. The enigma of the photograph containing vulgar portrait draws the readers into the vortex of suspense. The past relationship between Kamlesh and Prakash and the new romance between Ed (who is nobody else but Prakash) are masterly and beautifully counterpoised. In Sheridan's *The Rivals*, the hero, Captain Absolute, is disguised as Beverley, similarly here Ed and Prakash are the same person. This disguise creates suspense and draws astonishment from audience. Regarding the dramatic technique and thematic aspects of the play, John McRae observes: "Each act builds to a climax of revelations and self discoveries. By the end of the play, Ed is seen as the most pathetic and self-deluding of all the characters, but Kamlesh too deceives himself and exploits others (The Guard, for example). The photo of Ed and Kamlesh together becomes emblematic (again a typical Dattani touch) of all that was good in their love, but which has now turned or been turned against that love."[5]

If we minutely judge the various layers of the characters of this play, we notice that Sharad and Deepali are very comfortable with their sexuality. Sharad behaves and dresses in an exaggerated and affected way. He is a bit flaunting too. On the other hand Deepali is just the opposite. She is more restrained and stable. Bunny, the T.V. actor, behaves like a traditional Indian gay man. All the characters are brought together in such a way so as to expose the conflicts and repression, secrets and scandals. As a result "The audience must go through the classic cathartic emotions of terror and pity as the characters' masks fall, their emotions unravel and their lives disintegrate."[6]

The beauty of the book lies in its stage and symbols making the play very similar to Arthur Miller's. The title of the play is itself symbolic. In a muggy weather, the atmosphere is unpleasantly warm, damp and clammy and it makes us feel uncomfortable or tired. As a matter of fact, all the characters are feeling ill-at-ease and they want to set themselves free from suffocation, frustration and isolation. Though they look very nice outwardly, yet inwardly they are hollow and very tired. Ed, in the long run, attains his tragic grandeur in introspecting his life and in expressing his desire to live:

Sharad: Runs to the door and yells out). Guard! Guard! For God's sake somebody help!

Kiran! Somebody save him! He will kill my brother! No!

Ed: (Hits out at Kamlesh, crying with anger), Faggot! Pansy! Gandu! Gandu!

Sharad: (screaming). GUAAARD!

Ed: (Looks at Kiran). I am . . . sorry, I did not mean to harm you, I only wanted to live. (110)

At another place Ed repeats his desire to live—to live a life of an ideal social being free from the corruption of private life. He says: "Where do I begin? How do I begin to live? . . . Will you help me? What makes a man a man?" (111) The play ends with the self-discovery of Sharad. "I ask myself what have I got and what I am and what I'm not." (111)

Actually this is the mystery of man's hidden nature which the author wants to dig out through characterization and stage direction. In the stage direction we get a very telling symbol of 'fireworks' and a barat party. The image of 'fireworks' occurs again and again like the major images of Shakespearean tragedies. It seems to suggest the 'explosion of one's self.' As the drama runs, the characters are seen unmasking their hidden selves one by one. And their explosion of the self is beautifully suggested by the fireworks. In the end all characters come out with their true pictures. This is suggested by more and more fireworks: "More firecrackers and lusty yells from the wedding below." (111)

Firecrackers accompanied by coloured lights, yells and screams in the barat party enhance the symbolic effect and suggest tacitly the fuss and commotion of the inner heart of the characters: "There is an explosion of fireworks. A riot of coloured lights is seen through the window. There are loud screams of delight and whistles from the ground floor." (109) On another level, the fireworks, screams, yells and delights also suggest the wild and savage entertainment. The extraordinary fancy which Kamlesh develops from Ed reminds us of Marlowe's character Gaveston in *Edward II*. It is also very similar to Sheridan's characterization in *The Rivals*. In *The Rivals*, characters never realize their follies and drawbacks. But the characters of *On a Muggy Night in Mumbai* talk to their pious soul and realize their blunders. Like the tragic heroes of Shakespeare, they succeed in effecting tragic self-realization and thereby arouse a sense of pity and catharsis in the hearts of the readers or audience.

The psychological analysis of the various layers of unnoticed shades in the characters is worth noting. It recalls Virginia Woolf's famous lines: "Life is not a series of gig lamps symmetrically arranged, but a luminous halo, a semi-transparent envelope." Freud says that man's mind is like an iceberg whose major part lies hidden beneath the surface. Here in this drama also, we seldom see the truth in the beginning of the play. The 'face' and 'dress' of the characters seldom speak their real worth. It is their 'address' in the third act that reveals their hidden reality.

Final Solutions is a stage play in three acts. It deals with communalism, religious fanaticism and the Hindu-Muslim riot mostly engendered by the self-centred politicians. On the second level of meaning the play also suggests the deep-rooted hatred planted by our forefathers. The demons of hatred are not in the procession or on the street but they are sitting stably in our hearts. The playwright seems to fling a mild satire on those fanatics who don't understand the true property of religion, boast the merit of their religion and are mostly driven like dumb cattle by the egocentric and selfish politicians. In "A Note on the Play," Alyque Padamsee observes: "The mob in the play is symbolic of our own hatred and paranoia. Each member of the mob is an individual yet they meld into one seething whole as soon as politicians play on their fears and anxieties. . . . This is a play about transferred resentments. About looking of a scapegoat to hit out at when we feel let down, humiliated. Taking out your anger on your wife, children or servant is an old Indian custom."[7]

The issue which Dattani has raised in this play is not confined to only our land, but it has assumed a universal character. It is a confrontation between Arabs and Jews, whites and blacks, Hindus and Muslims, traditional and modern, and above all, between the innocent general people and crafty politicians. The author is in suspicion whether there is any final solution or not. He seems to be raising questions: "Is life a forward journey or do we travel round in circle, returning to our starting point? Can we shake off our prejudices or are they in our psyche like our genes? Will we ever be free or ever-locked in combat?" (173)

The beauty of the book lies in its excellent use of chorus, symbols and images. The play is full of animal images, very loathsome and fierce. It suggests the easily behaviour of the fanatics who have no religion as such. Let us see some of them:

> A lizard! It fell on the milk vessel. We will have to throw the milk away. (173)
>
> Well, that's because I think my lord and master has the brains of a silly goat. (173)

> Yes, there is a bad smell. Like a dead pig. (178)
> Drive them out! Kill the sons of swine. (178)
> Should we meld into anonymity so they cannot hound us? (196)
> Like the droning of bees around a hive. The humming grew louder until I could hear what they were chanting. (206)
> Mummy, thank you for making me feel like a rat in a hole. (210)
> Looking like a mouse in a family of cats. (218)

The image of 'mouse' and 'rat' suggests the fear and the strength in a group dominated society where people, if they are in majority, behave like cats, and if they are in minority, they prefer to hide in their hole like mice. Similarly, the image of 'swine' and 'dead pig' connote hatred and contempt. The dropping of a lizard on a milk vessel is supposed to be very inauspicious in the Hindu tradition. So, this image speaks volumes. The image of hunting dogs which is implied in the word 'hound' is very suggestive. It shows the ferocity of the fanatics of both the communities who go berserk with the fire of communal hatred and commit such heinous crimes which seldom behove an ideal humanity.

The extended metaphor of music, the music of Noor Jehan, Shamshad Begum and Suraiya, occurs in the play frequently. The music is interrupted by throwing of stone: "A stone hit our gramophone table, breaking it. Krishna chose to destroy what I loved most. My entire collection of records broken. Lying about like pieces of glass. Shamshad Begum, Noor Jehan, Suraiya. The songs of the love that I had learnt to sing with. Those beautiful voices cracked." (167)

Now the question arises: Why is it that the play is intertwined with music and that too, again and again. It connotes several layers of meaning. First, it shows how in life, music is needed to ease the savage blows of cruelty, conservatism and callousness, how despite various ups and downs life is as sweet and melodious as music; how music creates a sense of equality, fraternity and creativity in all men barring caste, class and creed. Music here also suggests religion which makes no distinction between the rich and the poor, the high and the low. The music of classical nature directly derives from the core of heart and it is enjoyed by each and all. Similarly, religion, in the true sense of the term, is very similar to music. All religions, however different they are in form, are one in spirit. All of them sing the same music of love, truth, humanity and fraternity. But there is communal hatred. They, it seems, represent the stones which break the music. At the end of the play, the author says. "The song plays for some time and stops as if the record has been smashed by a stone." (226) In the middle of the play also, the author repeats the same image which makes the metaphor more emphatic: "It ends abruptly with the sound of a stone breaking the record." (176)

The role of chorus in this play is also remarkable. Through chorus, the playwright seems to communicate to the audience the present scenario of communicable frenzy and hatred. Five people in the chorus do not belong to any religion and so ideally they wear black. The colour black is suggestive. No colour can be written or painted on the black. It shows justice and impartiality. There are five Hindu masks and five Muslim masks. The mob/chorus becomes the chorus when they 'wear' either the Hindu or the Muslim masks.

Well, through this beautiful technique of masking and unmasking the same person, the author seems to speak a lot of things. Religion is one; God is one; but the interpreters are different. When the people in the chorus wear the masks of the Hindu, they speak.

Chorus1: The procession has passed through these lanes Every year, for forty years.
Chorus 2, 3: How dare they?
Chorus 1,2, 3 For forty years our chariot has moved through their mohallas.
Chorus 1, 2, 3: Why did they? Why did they today?
Chorus 4, 5: Why did they? Why did they today?
Chorus 2, 3.: They broke our rath. They broke our chariot and felled our Gods.
Chorus 1, 2, 3: This is our land. How dare they?
Chorus 1: It is in their blood
Chorus 2, 3: It is in their blood to destroy!
Chorus 4: Why should they?

Chorus 5: It could have been an accident.

It is interesting to note here that except chorus 5, all the four are very jingoist and fanatic in their attitude. But chorus 5 speaks sense. Here it represents a few intellectuals of both communities who know the true meaning of religion and who believe in science. But unfortunately people seldom pay any heed to their views.

Now let us see an example of the Muslim chorus:

Chorus 1: Their chariot fell in our street!
Chorus: 2: Their God now prostrates before us!
Chorus: 3: So they blame it on us!
Chorus 1: Was the chariot built by us!
Chorus 2, 3: Blame the builder of those fancy thrones.
Chorus 4: A manufacturing defect!
Chorus 5: Doesn't their God have a warranty?
Chorus All: We are neither idol makers nor breakers?
Chorus 3. They say we razed their temples yesterday.
Chorus 2: That we broke their chariot today.
Chorus 1: That we'll bomb their streets tomorrow.
Chorus All: Why would we? Why ? Why? Why would we?
Chorus 5: (emotionally). Why would we?

Thus through this deft use of chorus, the dramatist wants to express the hidden thoughts of both communities. The author is neither with the Hindus nor with the Muslims. He is neutral.

Mahesh Dattani, in his preface to his *Collected Plays*, says that he is always confronted with remarks such as 'Your plays are preaching to the converted. You would do *Final Solutions* in the village." But the fact is, if his works are read and evaluated with the eyes of a judge, they look like fine examples of art. The author has no theory or principle to express and expose. He simply allows the play to run smoothly on the path of literature. The path is shadowed and decorated with the colourful trees and manifold flowers. In other words, it is his characters who speak, not the author. Dattani observes: "I also know that I have a lot to say and am probably not saying it well enough. But my characters have a lot to say too, and they seem to be doing rather well at having their say. . . . I am completely aware that it is my character that has done the work for me."[8]

Thus, this brief analysis of Mahesh Dattani's three plays shows that the author is bestowed with a special gift of fusing feeling with the form and thereby turning the play into art or in Eliot's terminology an Emotional Equivalent.

NOTES

1. http://www.anitanair.net/pages/profiles-md.htm
2. *Ibid.*
3. Michael Walling, "A Note on the Play," *Bravely Fought the Queen*, in *Collected Plays of Mahesh Dattani* (New Delhi: Penguin, 2000), p. 229.
4. Jeremy Mortimer, "A Note on the Play," *Seven Steps around the Fire*, in *Collected Plays of Mahesh Dattani*, p. 1.
5. John McRae, "A Note on the Play," *On a Muggy Night in Mumbai*, in *Collected Plays of Mahesh Dattani*, p. 44.
6. Ibid., p. 46.
7. Alyque Padamsee, "A Note on the Play," *Final Solutions*, in *Collected Plays of Mahesh Dattani*, p. 161.
8. Mahesh Dattani, "Preface," *Collected Plays of Mahesh Dattani*, p. xi.

Theatre: Reaching out to People
An Interview with Mahesh Dattani

SACHIDANANDA MOHANTY
University of Hyderabad

Mahesh Dattani stands out in a group of high profile critics and writers. Acclaimed as a leading playwright in English, he has bagged the Sahitya Akademi Award for his play *Final Solutions*. In an interview with Sachidananda Mohanty, the playwright-director spoke of his art and the state of theatre in India.

SM: How and when did you start writing plays?

MD: I began writing plays about ten years ago. It is an interesting story because I never really set out to be a playwright. I think very few say that they wish to be a playwright initially. I was involved in the theatre from a very young age, in the sense that although I didn't participate, I was attracted to the theatre.

SM: Where did you receive your early education?

MD: In Baldwin's School, Bangalore. Later, I studied at St. Joseph's College where I read History, Economics, Political Science. My interest in theatre sort of grew side by side in college. I became a member of a popular amateur theatre company called the "Bangalore Little Theatre." I used to do a lot of work such as backstage acting and stuff like that. Later, I moved on to directing plays.

SM: Can you mention some names?

MD: Yes. I did Sartre's play translated as *In Camera* and I produced the effect of Gamma rays in *The Man of the Moon*. Then an American play—all-female cast. Subsequently, I started my own theatre company and my first production was Hipolytes by Euripides. That didn't go down too well for various reasons. Next, I did a few comedies. Really light-hearted. At that point, I felt the need to do plays, Indian plays in English language. I wasn't entirely happy with the translation available, I felt that the language was stilted. It just didn't present any real speech; it was either far too academic or just did a literal translation of the original. So I felt that there ought to be more plays written originally in the English language. I decided to try my hand at it. That's how I began writing. After the first play, there has been no looking back. People accepted me. And as a result of doing Indian plays, my audience actually grew.

SM: What was your first play?

MD: It's called *Where There's a Will* and it's about this patriarch who controls his family—his wife, son and daughter-in-law. He dies at the end of the first scene, and his ghost becomes the narrator. What he has done is that he has left a very convoluted "Will" and his family had to act according to his wishes to inherit. The ghost is later exorcised by the women.

SM: Excellent! Now, Mahesh, drama as a genre is, in a sense, not very popular. At the same time, it remains one of the most powerful mediums. How does it feel to handle such a genre?

MD: Well, I think this is a wrong perception prevailing among the academics, especially the view that writing for the stage is inferior to writing a novel or writing poetry. I think it is important to keep in mind that the playwright is actually a craftsman. He is a "wright" and not "write." Sorry if I'm pontificating. . . .

SM: Not at all! Please go on.

MD: Well, I think it's more to do really with dramatic structure and less with literary skills. I think the skill of the playwright is listening to day-to-day speech and not making it sound flowery. At least I try to be different. I think it has more to do with understanding human relationships and how conflict can be presented on stage. I don't see it as less popular. For instance, even a serious play like *Final Solutions* had about forty shows in Bombay.

SM: Extraordinary!

MD: Yes. Maybe 25-30,000 people saw it. Now, I'm not sure what the readership of a novel in India would be!

SM: Okay. Looking back, Mahesh, what do you think have been your major achievements?

MD: I don't know whether I've had any significant achievements.

SM: You know you've been well received by the public that appreciates good theatre.

MD: Well, maybe the sheer fact that I'm projecting a milieu that is close to the audience—I think that may itself be an achievement. That's what makes my theatre alive.

SM: Can you remember some names of the plays that have become more successful?

MD: I think *Dance Like a Man* and *Tara* are the two plays that have been commercially the most successful.

SM: A few words about each of them.

MD: Okay! *Dance Like a Man*, this is during my Bharatnatyam days. It is about an old couple, dancers, ex-dancers. They are in their sixties and they are looking back at the past when they struggled against the stigma attached to Bharatnatyam in the fifties, that it was a *devadasi's* dance, compounding the problem for the man.

Tara is about a boy and a girl, Siamese twins. I have taken medical liberty over here because Siamese twins are invariably of the same sex and they are surgically separated at birth. It was important for their survival and the play deals with their emotional separation.

SM: How do you look at the Anglo-American theatre in this country? The theatre that has been traditionally presented in the English departments? Do you think such plays have any social or cultural relevance today?

MD: This definitely seems to be a problem. People get very upset when I say this. I think that this kind of cultural imitation reflects more a feeling of inferiority among the people who do it. I've been a victim of that as well. It's that you aspire to belong to a culture that is really not yours; it can never be yours. The cultural aspiration is actually projected by the way one does Anglo-American plays. I think it has nothing to do with theatre, it is a personal aspiration, a sad reflection of what kind of culture we value. We don't see this as any different from colonial inferiority. It's definitely a throwback on that. However, that does not negate the fact that there are people who are doing very good work using European or American plays.

SM: Would it, therefore, be accurate to describe the choice you've made in the field of Indian theatre as part of decolonisation?

MD: Again, I don't think I had such lofty political ideals when I began writing. I think it was a personal discovery because I too grew up with missionary or convent education. Of course, I was told that our art and culture were inferior to European culture. And there was a rebel in me, you know. I stopped reading Yeats and Shakespeare for a long time because I felt that I had enough of such stuff during my school days. I made an attempt to understand myself better and I guess this prompted me to do Indian plays.

SM: Mahesh, you have always attempted to depict in your plays the themes and concerns of everyday experience. What motivated you to take up such an approach?

MD: Well, again perhaps this is a projection of who I am. In America, playwrights are searching for things to talk about because everything has been done, and the audience has become blasé. But what is interesting here is that the blasé attitude is not there among the audience. I think there is so much happening today—gender equation and class-consciousness, for instance.

SM: What have been the modes that you have chosen for yourself? Has it always been the realistic mode, or have you attempted other modes such as the expressionistic, or the mythological, for instance?

MD: Again, I think the use of myths or legends has its own problems because you already have a mindset towards that. So what invariably might happen is that if you see yourself as a radical, you would try to pass an antithesis to popular myths or legends. Hopefully not? Or sometimes you might just project the same values that are there, knowingly or unknowingly. Supposing you did a play like *Liberation of Sita*, it amounts to sacrilege. And as for the other forms, I think it has a lot to do with the context.

As for realism, this may be true. I think realism is one of the forms that I use. Because of its popularity in the West, it continues to be relevant. It has got a new lease of life due to television. Playwrights are writing realistic scripts for the stage in order to get accepted. I see realism as one of the forms that

I've made use of. I've used the chorus as a narrative device, and I've used time and space in different ways in my plays. I think all the tools of theatre are available to a playwright and you just use them the way your sensibility allows you to use them.

SM: Who has had a major influence on your art?

MD: Well, I was particularly impressed by the plays of Vijay Tendulkar. Actually, that was one of the reasons why I decided to write myself, because when I saw plays in Hindi or Gujarati and I managed to acquire the translation, they just didn't have the same impact. *Silence, the Court is in Session!* was such a brilliant play, but I felt that the translation in English threw away most of the effect. Later on, it was Tennessee Williams. I relate to Tennessee Williams because he writes about vulnerable women in a very violent society. I think I tend to do that as well, although I don't see my woman as vulnerable, in the sense that they do fight their battles. They are not on the winning side of the battle, and I think I have learnt a lot about dramatic structure.

SM: What has been your understanding of Gujarati plays? I understand that Gujarati is your mother tongue. I'm sure that you had some acquaintance with Gujarati theatre. What would you think is the current stage of Gujarati theatre and how do you relate it to Marathi theatre?

MD: It's like chalk and cheese. I feel that Marathi theatre is far more sophisticated and in the mainstream, whereas Gujarati theatre tends to be classic. Gujarati theatre has a very strong following; Marathi has no less, but the kind of stuff that is put on the Gujarati stage leaves a lot to be desired. I won't even call some of it as theatre.

SM: Slapstick?

MD: Even if it was slapstick well done, I think that would be good theatre. It's just that it's a very weak plot; most of it is just plagiarised West-End or Broadway sex comedy. They throw in a lot of topical jokes, and there is no dramatic effect. I don't think the audience is looking for that. It's just melodrama blue. At the worst, it is just a series of blue jokes. I think the only group that's doing something worthwhile, perhaps, is the Indian National Theatre, where they do Marathi and Gujarati plays. They have a long tradition of being slightly more political. They have revived Bhavai and done some interesting things. The rest of it, at least to my knowledge, is pure junk. Some of the good stuff that has come out of Gujarati theatre like *Gandhi Virodh Gandhi* is actually adaptations of the original Marathi plays. The good stuff is from the Marathi theatre.

SM: How did you conceive of a play like *Final Solutions*, which is based on the issue of fundamentalism, and in particular, the destruction of Babri Masjid? How did you think of it?

MD: Well, I wrote the plays before the destruction of the Babri Masjid, when the Ram Janmabhoomi was an issue in Parliament. I was commissioned to write that play by Alyque Padamsee. Initially I was hesitant.

SM: What is the main structural outline of the play?

MD: It's about two Muslim boys running away from a mob and seeking shelter in a Hindu household. Now, it transpires that they know the girl who lives there. The prejudices of the family are brought to the forefront. There is, of course, a façade of being liberal-minded.

SM: *The Third Reich and the Holocaust*! Is that where the title came from?

MD: Yes, exactly!

SM: Mahesh, how do you look at the current state of the Indian-English theatre?

MD: Well, there definitely is more prolific maturity in the cities. Some of it good and some bad. . . . However, there is now a definite focus on Indian plays that try to embody the kind of values and aspirations I've been talking about. I do see this effort as breaking fresh ground. There is more money in English language theatre than in any other theatre in the country, and I feel that it is moving in the right direction. Again, the problem is how to maintain a standard—because almost all the English language theatre in our country is amateur; very few people actually have formal training. I think that's what we need to focus on now.

SM: What do you think can be done to make theatre more accessible to the people?

MD: Unless you reflect the ethos of the people, it is going to be an elitist theatre; or it is going to be a museum piece intended to satisfy curiosity. On the other hand, if you widen your audience, the only thing you can do is to write more about them.

SM: What are your views about the patronage of the theatre in India by business houses that, of course, have their own interests?

MD: Well, it's a mixed blessing. In a sense, there is more money available. There are strings attached, no doubt! You have to do something that they feel is right for the image of the company. It's like taking one step forward and two steps backward. The money is available and so we feel there is a chance to do more theatre. You are taking two steps backward because the kind of theatre you are doing, for instance, say . . .

SM: Neil Simon comedies?

MD: Yes. Or a musical like *My Fair Lady*. I don't see the point in doing that. I think the corporate houses need to look at their own images. They are anxious to project a Westernised image. That way, they are losing the market. The successful ones are those that have captured the national spirit. Just look at the "Hamara Bajaj" ad, for instance. It might be corny, but it captures the sentiment of the masses. Then there are the other corporate houses, the banks and the mobiles, for instance. I think it's quite stupid—if they want to capture a wider section of the market, they have to reflect its ethos. Unfortunately, in the advertising field, at the top of the corporate world, people have a . . .

SM: Western mindset?

MD: Yes, exactly! It's silly. It's bad marketing policy, really.

SM: Although you are eminently qualified, you have chosen to be a freelancer. Do you find this situation congenial for your creative work?

MD: You know, to the theatre practitioner, it's a full-time job. You have to be mad to be able to do it! Maybe I have that kind of madness because I could easily be doing something boring and earning a lot. But then, would that not kill me?

Conversing with Mahesh Dattani

RANU UNIYAL
Lucknow University, Lucknow

One of the leading Indian English playwrights, Mahesh Dattani is a winner of Sahitya Akademi Award. His is a voice of the marginalized. Asserting the identity, aspirations and anxieties of those on the periphery Dattani looks at theatre as a collective experience. Each of his plays has a certain open-endedness about it which compels the audience to pause, reflect and question.

RU: Could you tell me something about your background?

MD: Well, I grew up in Bangalore and my parents are from Gujarat and they moved to Bangalore many years ago. It must have been 50 yrs ago and they liked the place and stayed on and so I do feel attached to Bangalore. I received my education in Bangalore and I guess like a lot of other middle-class families who felt the importance of English—that their children should have an English language education so that they can interact cross-culturally and so my parents put me in a school that was known for its standard of English, I guess and so that decided the language I was going to operate in later on in my life.

RU: Did you use Gujarati as your first language at all?

MD: My mother tongue is Gujarati. My Mom doesn't know English and even with my Dad I conversed in Gujarati (my father passed away in 2000) and it's only amongst the siblings, my two sisters and I, that we speak in English because all three of us received an education where the first language, that is, the medium of instruction was English, and of course, we were encouraged to speak in English at a very young age because that was seen as the language of the future.

RU: And then we cannot deny history and its impact on us.

MD: Absolutely. That's right, because it is in our mindsets that people who do speak English come from a particular educated background because education and the English language are synonymous now in our country. Fortunately or unfortunately, that's the reality.

RU: First you started as an actor, later you moved on to direction?

MD: That's right. And I guess, I have been interested in theatre right from the beginning, from a very early age. And I began acting in plays and then I moved on to directing.

RU: And then to writing plays.

MD: That's right, because writing plays really happened more out of necessity because I wanted to do more Indian plays in English. But the translations that were available didn't do justice to the original. So I thought why not try my hand in writing the plays myself and it's quite ironic that what I began to do out of necessity became a passion. Later I had my theatre company in Bangalore and at the moment a studio theatre just two streets from where I live devoted entirely to new writing in English. And I do workshops for playwrights and actors and directors as well and I see it as a laboratory for new works, interesting new works.

RU: How did you plan out your stage?

MD: The studio, well, that came about from my travels abroad especially in England where I did see that the mainstage theatres did have what they call a black box studio theatre. Basically it's a large room, black and that's how the name black box came about. And they've got 50 seats or at the most 100. It's very flexible and you get to do some very interesting stuff there which may not receive a mainstream audience. But at the same time that is important work and that kind of work needs to be done. Also the other thing that an intimate space like that provides is that the audience has the luxury of viewing or experiencing the performance from real close. The performance space and then audience space, there is very little demarcation between the two, so that is a speciality. I think of intimate small scale theatre spaces and that's a concept that I think hasn't really caught on in India and I see the future of a lot of theatre lies in these smaller spaces because the mainstage has its limitations and what we really need are smaller spaces. But out in the suburbs especially a city like Bangalore which is spread out and tends to be sort of moving outwards, because it's not an island like Mumbai that there is a limitation of land, it just keeps spreading you know and absorbing. Such concepts do add on to the quality of drama.

RU: And sense of space is obviously something which is very important as far as theatre is concerned.

MD: Yes, I think so and we need to reconfigure that space because again it's a British legacy, this tradition of conventional stage where the action is sort of removed from the audience by way of a formal stage and a curtain. It is not that I'm doing anything new. If you look at our folk theatre and even especially in the south, Kathakali, they were done in the fields and the torches would demarcate the boundaries of performance space and the audiences would sit around that and so in that sense it is not new to our tradition but it is definitely new to our generation which have now developed.

RU: Well in several parts of North India we still have the Nautanki and the Ramleela which is out in the open and it is from among the people that the actors come up. It is being done at a very modest scale by people who are interested in the traditional art form. And also by those who are interested in the religious aspect of it.

MD: Of course, I think that's the beauty of traditional theatre that it is so associated with religion because theatre was used as a way of preserving religion and the tales of the epics. Ramleela was a perfect example and that's somehow kept our culture alive. But of course, what I am talking about is really cutting-edge theatre or radical theatre which questions existing values and challenges people with what they consider the norm.

RU: Your writing seems very radical. Eunuchs, gays, victims of child abuse, alternate sexuality—you seem to have a passion for the marginalized?

MD: Ya, I guess so. Because I do see myself as very contemporary and I do see the clashes of the old and the new in our society and especially on a familial level, on a societal level. We are talking about communal complex, we're talking about gender battles maybe and the male-female equation have been re-examined, at least in the cities. And I think all this has to reflect in the theatre we do, and it's absolutely vital and necessary for this to happen.

RU: Do you relate to the work of someone like Vijay Tendulkar or is there a generation gap?

MD: I do relate to Vijay Tendulkar because when he began writing plays about middle class values and challenging them, I think he was a little ahead of his times in the 60s and 70s and I think his plays still have resonancy today and so I think, I don't see a generation gap.

RU: You think theatre should be ahead of its time.

MD: I think it should be.

RU: Or is it all about the changing times?

MD: I think it is all about reflecting the time which we are in and if those times are changing then I think that it needs to be reflected in the theatre. If the things aren't changing then even that needs to be reflected.

RU: Well, one thing that we see is that Shakespeare goes down very well with Indian audiences, isn't it? Does familiarity have anything to do with popularity? Under-graduates, people in school are familiar with Shakespeare.

MD: Yes and also, Shakespeare does move with times, I think.

RU: He is ahead of his times.

MD: That's right. I think, even if you look at something like *Othello* it is such a powerful subject.

RU: *Hamlet*?

MD: *Hamlet*, yes, the entire dilemma of taking action and you know plays like *Romeo and Juliet*, you could set that in a Hindu-Muslim situation and it'll be extremely relevant today.

RU: You mean relocation is an important device?

MD: Yes, I think this relocation is something which theatre offers, that is, if you could take even a Greek tragedy and relocate it to present-day socio-political situation, whatever you want and I think that is what makes a play a classic is that it may have its form, it may have its structure, some of it may be antiquated, but in essence it is timeless and universal as well.

RU: What is theatre according to you? How do you rate it next to fiction or to poetry as far as literature is concerned?

MD: I think, of all the arts and of all the writing genres, theatre perhaps is the most dynamic because no other art form is as vibrant.

RU: It is the most flexible and delightfully challenging of all art forms.

MD: I think so, yes, because the kind of chemistry that can be created between audience and performer on a very immediate, on a gut level, I don't think any other genre offers that and I think that is what makes it very valuable tool, as an agent of social change maybe without being didactic or whatever.

RU: Preachy?

MD: Yes, without being preachy and at the same time as a very raw form of communication, and it need not have a very special language, the way classical dance does or opera or classical music does where it is the privilege of a few who understand the language of that genre. Whereas theatre can be appreciated by anyone, the most uneducated person by any standard of our society could relate to it as much as the most educated.

RU: You just referred to your interest in ballet and you were a dancer as well.

MD: I used to dance

RU: Bharatnatyam?

MD: Bharatnatyam, yes.

RU: So how do you link dance with drama—is one complementing the other?

MD: Yes, it does. On a very basic, technical level, it does. I haven't really made a conscious effort of using the language of Bharatnatyam in theatre. Although I do not rule that out, I might do it at a later stage, I haven't done it as yet.

RU: You could experiment with it.

MD: I could, yes, that's right, it's a possibility that's open to me and I would have the equipment to deal with that having had an extensive training in Bharatnatyam and some training in Western ballet as well. I guess, all the performing arts are definitely related and again it's not anything new to our culture because if you look at traditional theatre, dance, drama and music are integrated.

RU: Are you happy with your response to *The Final Solution*?

MD: Yes, I am, in fact, beyond expectation. When I first did that play, I didn't expect it to do so well. I just thought that it would have a few shows, there might be a select audience that might be interested in that sort of thing and that's it. But it has reached to a great deal of people which I find very reassuring that a subject which is awkward, a subject that is very delicate, very volatile, very sensitive can be viewed with a distance in the theatre again. Like I mentioned that theatre can affect you on a very raw level but at the same time it offers a distance which opens up other possibilities, other ways of viewing things.

RU: Could you talk about *The Final Solution*? What is it about?

MD: It is basically, dramatically, about two Muslim boys running away from a mob that is out to kill them and they seek shelter in a Hindu household, seemingly liberal-minded and their presence through the night triggers off memories for the matriarch, the older woman, the grandmother.

RU: Daksha.

MD: Daksha, yes, and you do see Daksha as a young bride and through her diary and her narration.

RU: In her is a voice wanting to write all the time, speak out.

MD: Absolutely and what Daksha has is her diary and through the device of the diary, she begins a dialogue with the audience and that is the only space that is offered to Daksha because she can make fun of her in-laws, she could talk very honestly about her feelings, about her friendship with the Muslim girls etc. directly to the audience and that space is denied to her with the other members of her household including her husband and these are memories that she has retained even in her old age and these memories are triggered off and feelings of prejudice that had developed over the years are brought out in the present day situation. So Daksha becomes a symbol of our historical vision, our sense of history, how prejudice is formed and how we deal with the situation today.

RU: Did you move on to theatre soon after your graduation?

MD: Well, yes I did. Even in college, I did a fair amount of theatre with an amateur theatre company in Bangalore called the "Bangalore Little Theatre" and I continued with my interest over the years after I graduated. These days my theatre studio "Playpen" in Bangalore conducts theatre workshops on acting, play writing and directing.

RU: Could you tell me more about your other plays?

MD: Well, the other play which I think I could talk about is *Dance Like a Man* which is because we talked about my Bharatnatyam background. It is about Bharatnatyam dancers. Again in their old age, when they are in their 60s and they are looking back on to their struggling days, when they had their ideals and in the 50s where there was a stigma attached to the dance form; that it is a dance form of the Devdasis, it's a prostitute's dance and people from respectable families didn't perform or practice that dance form. It is doubly difficult for the man, you know, what business does a man have learning a prostitute's dance. So it brings about gender roles, what is expected of genders as well. And also the tensions between the couple and how they solve, how they felt that they used their relationship to develop their careers, dances and how they reconcile to the fact that the time wasn't right for them.

RU: When you write, do you have the audience in mind? Or do you have certain issues in mind? Well, how do you begin?

MD: That's a very complex question and it is very difficult for me to answer because anything can trigger off. Like, for instance *Bravely Fought the Queen* was triggered off by the poem we learnt in school, 'Khoob ladi mardani woh to Jhansi wali Rani thi' and what I had witnessed at somebody's house, was some form of battle between the woman and her husband and immediately something triggered off and the poem came to my mind, that she was fighting very bravely. And then I immediately got this setting of a woman fighting a losing battle and the title just came to me and is reflective of Laxmi Bai's fight against the British and it was a losing battle but she never gave up.

RU: Do you think you owe a certain responsibility to the society?

MD: Well, I do. But I could write a play that's totally frivolous and it would still be good theatre.

RU: And it would still go down very well with the audience?

MD: Yes, of course, but I think there are so many things, tensions, and conflicts that we're dealing with, that's what is my inspiration I'm not saying I'm committed, therefore, I'm writing about these issues, I'm writing because these issues are inspiring to me.

RU: And you feel strongly about them.

MD: That's right, I guess I do so. There are these recurring issues in my plays basically to do with gender inequality, the battle between the genders or in egalitarian position. The individual versus society, I guess, is a theme that's in all my plays.

RU: How do you look at the contemporary drama in English?

MD: Well, there is a dearth of playwrights in English.

RU: An important figure is Girish Karnad. He did a couple of them in English.

MD: Yes, that's right, he doesn't see himself as a writer of English language plays because he writes them in Kannada first and he has the capacity to translate them in English himself so he has a distinct advantage there and it's a wonderful thing that he is doing it. He's doing an important work which is very expansive and very high on ideology and with a sense of history. His interpretation of mythology is interesting. But I really hope that we have more new, young reasonable voices coming out and that's what the studio theatre is for.

RU: Do you see anyone around?

MD: Definitely there is talent. Well, back home there is Gautam Raja, who's a very young playwright. He's written a couple of full-length plays. And I think they're of a very good standard and I think he's one of our most promising young playwrights and there are established playwrights like Poyli Sengupta who writes, feels very strongly about women's issues and she's written some really strong and dynamic plays which have been performed in Bangalore and in Chennai and then there is, in Delhi, Manjula Padmanabhan who won an award and the kind of work she's doing is just as important. But again, in the cities, one can name two or three.

RU: Not a considerable body as such.

MD: No, it isn't and we need more.

RU: What else have you been working on?

MD: Well, I've done five Radio plays for BBC. Film "Mango Souffle" based on a play *On a Muggy Night in Mumbai* was nominated for the Commonwealth Film festival. Latest film "Morning Raga" is likely to be released soon. I also directed *Seven Steps around the Fire* in New Delhi. My studio has been functioning for the past seven years and has produced writers and actors, some of whom are doing well like Anupama Chandrashekhar, Vijay Nair and Kishwar Ahluwalia.

RU: It's really been nice talking to you. Very informative and I enjoyed the discussion.

MD: I did too.

RU: And I hope we meet again.

MD: Yes I hope so.